I Trained My Dog

&

He Still Won't Listen...

What Do I Do Now?

by Duane Overturf

Table Of Contents

Introduction

This book has been 6 years in the writing and over 30 years in the making. More than 6,000 dogs and their owners have contributed to the information you will read in this book. My goal when I set out to write a book about the training of dogs was to tell it like it really is in layman's terms so that anyone could understand it, even if they had never had a dog before in their life. I also did not want to do another "how-to" type of dog training book, that has been done, and there are some very good ones out there. Rather, I wanted to give people who have worked hard at teaching their dog themselves, or paid someone else to teach their dog, the missing information they needed to get their already trained dog to listen much better if not flawlessly.

The information in this book will help just about anyone with a dog, but people with dogs that are particularly difficult will be amazed at the changes they will see in their dog as they begin to apply and implement the exercises and suggestions I make throughout the book. You see, teaching your dog what you want them to do and getting your dog to listen to you with great reliability are two completely different things and they should not be confused with each other. In my more than 30 years of training family dogs and their families, I have discovered that in almost every case where a person has made an effort to train their dog, the dog really has learned what they want them to do, regardless of the "technique" they used to do it (I am not speaking about young puppies here. I am speaking about dogs that are coming out of their puppy hood and dogs that are already adults). The problem isn't that the dog doesn't understand. The problem is that the dog has never been given a reason to listen in a way that makes sense to him so every time he is asked to do something, he does it because he understands it is the best choice of all the options that are available to him at that moment.

This is not to say that I don't have a style or technique of training that I prefer over another. Perhaps the subject of another book in the future will be about my preferred techniques when I train and why I do it the way that I do.

Instead, this book is about you, the owner, and how your actions are very possibly undermining your efforts at having a highly responsive dog that you can truly enjoy rather than feel frustrated about. It is about how dogs learn and interpret what we do down to the smallest details. Things you might not even realize you are doing even though you think you are paying close attention to what you are doing. Hopefully, you will get the information you need to get your dog listening to your satisfaction. But you must realize that getting the information you need isn't enough. You must apply what you learn here to see the difference.

I want to thank all of my clients over the years who have helped to make this book possible, especially the 4 legged, and the occasional 3 and 2 legged ones, (dogs and people). I also want to thank those dog's families who hired me to help them over the years. All of them have been invaluable in teaching me what I needed to learn to pass this information along to people who live too far away to hire me directly.

Most of all, I want to thank my wife, Catherine, who has stood by me through this process every step of the way, and my daughter, Lindsay, who has given me new inspiration to stop procrastinating and finish writing it. Finally, I want to thank, Boscoe, Tia, Angel, Dayme, Tippy, Gretchen, Amber, Grigio, Jaeger, Frosty, Shiloh and Bianca. These wonderful dogs were my primary teachers and I owe much to them.

Chapter One

Who Really Needs Training?

I recently received a call from a distraught man and his wife. They were begging me to come over to their house immediately. They wanted me to get their dog off of their bed. They explained to me that earlier that day they had given their dog a meat bone to chew. Their dog then promptly jumped up on their bed to "have at it". Realizing that the bone was going to cause a mess on their comforter, they asked the dog to get off the bed. The dog however, had other plans. He wasn't about to give up such a prime spot so easily. When the man or his wife tried a little harder to get their dog to move, he growled, rushed at them quickly, and then returned to his bone when they backed off. After the first time this happened, they left the room to leave him alone for a while thinking that it would be easier a little bit later. This proved not to be the case. Each time they tried to move him off of the bed, he growled with more intensity and rushed at them with more vigor than before. It was now late in the afternoon and their dog had been in their room since morning.

I asked the man if this had ever happened before and he admitted it had, but not to the degree they were experiencing this time. When I told the man that I wouldn't come over just to get the dog off their bed, he was disappointed. I explained that the problem was bound to repeat itself in some way or another even if they didn't give the dog bones again. That this problem stemmed from a lack of appropriate leadership in the house and without him and his wife making some changes in the way they dealt with their dog, someone might eventually get hurt. This man even agreed this was likely to be true, but I never heard from him again.

I regularly get calls from people with similar problems. One call I received was about a toy poodle that would not let a man back into bed with his wife if he got up in the middle of the night to use the restroom. So this man was forced to lie miserable in bed with a full bladder or go sleep the rest of the night on the couch after getting up.

It amazes me how much people will put up with before calling for help. It amazes me even more when they still don't do anything about the situation. Problems like these are very common and can end up being quite serious, not to mention how much tension there must be for people to live in a home where their dog is calling the shots. These and many other problems are not really "dog" problems as much as they are "people" problems. The dogs in the above situations were probably not little terrorists in fur. More likely, they were simply doing what had worked on a smaller scale in the past to move up in status in the household. And since it worked in the past, they kept doing it. Dogs are very good at following the rule, "If it isn't broke don't fix it." As time goes by, dogs that are allowed to continue behaving like the one above using "dog language", as I like to call it, to manipulate situations may cause a real problem one day. Imagine when a child or unsuspecting person, who doesn't understand what the dog is trying to say, comes too close and gets bitten.

Dogs are becoming more and more popular as pets and are finding their way into homes of people that have little or no experience training them. This might even be the case with you. The most common mistake people make is to treat their dog as if they were people. But sometimes the calls I get are from people who have had many dogs in the past and for some reason, the dog they have now is not responding to their leadership the way their prior dogs did. I regularly get calls from people who say things like, "This is the fourth Cocker Spaniel

I've had and none of the other ones were like this" or "I've had dogs all my life and none of them gave me this much trouble."

With the exception of young puppies, I would have to say in 90% or more of the homes I visit, the dog(s) understand exactly what they are being asked to do. But does this mean a dog should respond just because it understands the command? To answer this question let me ask you a question. Do you do everything everybody asks you to do? My guess is you don't. I would be willing to bet that you decide on a case by case basis. Taking it a step further, I would also bet that in cases where you do respond every time by doing what someone asks, one of two factors exist. The first factor would be that the person doing the asking has the ability to carry out a consequence that matters to you, such as your boss at work has the ability to pay you or fire you. The second factor that might be present is the person doing the asking has earned your respect. Many times I'll bet you find that both of these elements are present.

Over the years, my own training methods have changed dramatically. But no matter how much my methods have changed, the dogs have always been able to learn what I was teaching them. Most of the time they learn it with great ease. If your dog is not listening to you, the problem is probably not that your dog hasn't learned what the commands mean. Most likely the problem is that your dog is choosing not to listen or to listen on a case by case basis just as you would do in the absence of

9

at least one of those two factors. The truth is, we all have our own agenda. Dogs, you, and every other living thing on the planet, have an agenda of their own. The trick in getting your dog to listen to you every time you ask is to make your agenda their agenda. In other words, to move listening to you to the top of their priority list. This can be done in more than one way.

Throughout this book you will learn ways to shift responsibility to your dog so that listening becomes important to them, regardless of whether or not you have a treat in your hand or what might be going on across the street at the moment. You will learn what appropriate leadership is and how to establish yourself as higher status than your dog in your family pack. You will also learn how to create a language that promotes a high degree of reliability in terms of your dog listening to commands. When you combine appropriate leadership with a language that is specifically designed to get your dog to listen without questioning you, you will have great control over your dog's actions and be well on the road to having a great relationship with your dog.

Some of the methods I recommend will be easy to implement while others may be more difficult for any number of reasons. For instance, you may have a physical handicap which prevents you from doing something I suggest, or a suggestion may require you to change your own habits. Since we don't know what will make the most difference to your individual dog, it is important to try and implement as many of the suggestions as possible. If something I suggest makes you think to yourself "I could never do that," I strongly urge you to try and gradually implement the suggestion until you become comfortable with it. I usually find the most difficult suggestions will make the most difference. Who knows, you might even find it helps you in other areas of your life as well. It wouldn't be the first time I heard a client make that comment.

There is a lot of discussion and argument among trainers about how a dog should be trained. Some organizations that are dedicated to teaching dog trainers new methods to train basic behaviors would also like to dictate what tools we are allowed to use in training. The push is towards using what is commonly being referred to as "dog-friendly" techniques. Still other organizations focus more on end results than on what technique or tools should or should not be used. I belong to a couple of these organizations and find them to be invaluable in helping further my knowledge. If trainers keep an open mind, we can all learn from each other. I will be the first to admit that my involvement in these organizations has been helpful in getting me to think outside of the box. When working with a dog that is not quick to respond to one method, it is helpful to know another way to get the job done.

Hopefully, as you read this you will keep an open mind about my suggestions as well. This book is the result of 30 years of focusing on training family dogs specifically. I have personally worked with approximately 6,000 dogs and their families over those years. My greatest teachers during that time have been the dogs and families I've worked with. Along the way, mistakes were made right along with the successes. I, myself, am always learning and closely observing what's going on between a client and their dog whenever they interact. I continue to learn from them and on occasion, a dog still humbles me. This is a good reminder that I still don't know it all, even after 30 years.

The recent push towards dog friendly training methods is having a two-prong effect. On the one hand it is moving training in the direction of more humane methods and I am the first to admit that this is a good thing. However, like any good thing, too much of it can be a bad thing. I believe that this is happening in the business of dog training. I am not referring to dog training for fun and sport here. I am specifically referring to the business of family dog training. People who are involved in dog sports are a different breed of person (pardon the pun) than the average family that brings home a Golden Retriever puppy for their kids. Most of the people that are involved in some kind of dog sport have, and are willing to commit, more time to training than an average mother with kids has available to her. A good percentage of these dog sport enthusiasts have decided that they don't want to have kids and that their dogs are their "kids." Many of these trainers begin teaching the public how to train their family dog out of their love for training and dogs. With the best of intentions they teach their clients using the methods that have worked for them in training their dog in a specific dog sport such as agility, or flyball. Usually, these methods strive to be as positive as possible. The problem with this is that the real world isn't an all-positive place. I'm not saying that these methods don't work. What I'm saying is that these methods require a much greater degree of time and devotion to training than the average mother with human kids has available to her. In many homes it simply isn't practical to expect the dog owner to devote as much time to training as the dog enthusiast has to devote to training their own dog.

The world is a fine balance between oppositions. Without the balance between positive and negative in training, results come much more slowly and many times not at all. Methods that work fine or even excellent among the people who are dog enthusiasts may have far less success in the home of the average family. One reason for this is that an "all-positive" approach requires a much greater level of skill and time to learn on the part of the trainer. Some methods can take years to master well; much longer than a person with a problem dog is willing to wait for results. Training away the bad habits using all positive methods requires a great time commitment that the average family simply does not have. Then, when training is not working so well, or the course is over and the client still has a dog with big problems, some of these trainers condemn the person for getting a dog in the first place. Reprimanding the owner, since they can't devote the same quantity of time to train their new puppy that the trainer had committed to training their own dogs. Often, they tell them they should never have gotten a dog because they don't have the time to devote to training. I've had more people than I can count call me on the phone crying because the last trainer they talked to or hired said they shouldn't have a dog for this exact reason.

I recently had a married couple as clients that had two German Shepherds. The first was a 2 year old male and the second was a 6 month old female. The older male had been through numerous group courses given at a local pet store. He was a smart dog that had learned a great deal of fun tricks in the classes he had gone through, but he had other issues that the training wasn't addressing. When people would visit this families home the dog was unpredictable. For instance, if someone would make a kissy noise with their lips to invite him over to see them he would go ballistic; like he was going to tear you apart. The family would caution visitors that they should not get up to walk around the house to get a glass of water or go to the bathroom without alerting one of the family members to escort them because it would set him off. After numerous classes the problem was not any better and now their new puppy was beginning to show the same behaviors, learning them from the older dog. When the couple took their new puppy to the trainer they had been using the trainer chastised them for getting another dog from the same breeder that the older dog came from. The trainer blamed the breeder for breeding dogs with unstable personalities. Finally, the couple decided to look elsewhere for help and called me. They got a second dog from this breeder because they loved the first dog in spite of his sketchy behavior. When I came into their house I could immediately sense the tenseness of the home as they told me to have a seat and be still. The dogs were barking aggressively at me and made me feel a bit uneasy. Not knowing about the kissy noise problem I made the noise to invite the dogs over to see me and they went berserk to the point they were almost uncontrollable by the couple. After getting some background information about the dogs and the training they were doing up to this point I laid out a plan to balance out their approach and desensitize the dogs to the noises and other stimuli that would set them off. They had created a fairy-tale world for their dogs were there were no consequences for inappropriate behavior, but plenty of consequences for good behavior. Unfortunately, many problem behaviors have rewards (positive consequences) built into them without us interfering. If we ignore these types of behaviors they usually will not go away no matter how much we try to reward other things to take their place. To help this couple

I had them implement virtually everything I outline in this book. Positive results could be seen almost immediately. Over the course of several months we worked together and today their dogs are much calmer, trustworthy and responsive to the couple even when distracted. The problem wasn't the breeding behind the dogs, the problem was a faulty approach to training that didn't balance the positive stuff they had learned with negative consequences for inappropriate behavior. The two dogs are still quite protective of the house when the couple are not home but are now able to better judge how to behave when they are home. The couple recently had a major remodel done to their house and during those several months of having workers in and out nearly every day they had no problems whatsoever. Even when they accidentally had a worker walk into their backyard alone and the couple were not around the dogs were okay. They went back to their previous trainer later and showed them the difference a little discipline made in their dogs. Unfortunately, it probably didn't make any difference. Some trainers will always be more concerned with being politically correct than they are with getting a problem solved and saving a dogs life. When picking a trainer be careful to ask enough questions that you screen out those trainers who advocate that certain tools should be banned or that they never use them, or those who claim to be all positive in their approach to training

Over the last 10 years I have seen a cross over

happening. People who are dog enthusiasts, and have fun competing in dog sports, are going into the business of dog training and giving advice about training family dogs. I have no problem with this; there is enough business out there for everyone. But underneath the surface, there is a real problem developing. Dogs are being turned in to shelters and dog pounds at an increasing rate. Huge numbers of these dogs have already been through a training program where the focus was to stay politically correct according to standards published and taught by some of these organizations.   They focus on the rules of training instead of focusing on getting the job done which will ensure a long healthy life with the family.

One organization I belong to has put together a written exam where anyone that wants to can pay a fee to take the exam and with a little bit of book study, pass it and become "certified" as a pet dog trainer. These titles may be very confusing to an unknowing public because it gives the impression that a person has experience training where in reality the person may not have ever trained a dog in their life. The extent of their knowledge and experience may be 100% out of a book. How scary is that? I am not knocking this organization here. I have learned new information attending seminars they offer at their annual meeting and through their newsletters. I just don't agree that passing a written exam is a good way to judge a trainer's ability. After reading this book you could probably pass that exam yourself.

   The other prong of this push towards dog-friendly methods is that it may be doing a disservice to dogs by sending them to an early grave. Dogs that could have otherwise lived a happy life if the trainer were more flexible in their methods and taught the owner an approach that would have worked more quickly; not to mention the message it sends to kids and the emotions it brings up in a family when the decision to get rid of the dog is made. Is it the fault of the people who brought the dog home or the fault of the trainer that was hired to help and didn't teach their clients how to gain control of their dog quickly enough to save the dogs life? I have had many clients over the years that had been through training with another trainer and did not even complete the lessons because progress was so slow or who finished a course only to immediately hire me because the first course didn't help them in the way they hoped. Admittedly, I have failed a few clients over the years myself when I didn't recognize how close the dog was to getting a one way ticket to the pound. My own failure to notice this is one of the factors that has caused me to evaluate anew how I will approach training each dog and family whose home I walk into. There is nothing worse than the feeling that you failed a client because you didn't give them the answers that would give results fast enough.

   If 90% of the homes I walk into have adult dogs that

understand what is being asked of them and they are choosing not to listen, then who needs the training? The answer is that the people do. Training is at least 50% training the people if not much more. Over the years my methods have evolved into what they are today and they will continue to evolve over time as I learn new ways to approach training and incorporate the new knowledge that keeps flowing forth from these wonderful organizations. This may sound like a contradiction but I really have to thank all those dog-sport enthusiasts for things they discover that can be applied to family dog training. I am not condemning them at all. In fact, I give them high praise for their work.

The first time I saw a clicker training demonstration I was very skeptical about how I could use this training tool with my clients. To make me even more skeptical the person doing the demonstration would not answer any of my questions about how they use a clicker to solve a behavioral problem. But I saw something in the demonstration that caught my interest enough to lead me to experiment with this tool and do more research on how to use it. Today I use a clicker with nearly every puppy I am called upon to help train and on some of the adult dogs too. Do I think it's the greatest thing since sliced liver? No, to me it's just another tool I have at my disposal to use which aids in the learning process.

Some of what you read in this book will be considered

controversial. Given the wide range of opinions about how a dog should be trained, some of the trainers that read this book will give it high praise while others will call some of my suggestions cruel and inhumane. There is a joke among dog trainers that if you get 3 trainers together the only thing that 2 of them can agree on is that the 3rd trainer is doing it wrong. Since I did not write this book for trainers or the organizations out there I am not concerned with being politically correct. If my suggestions help keep dogs in their home that would otherwise have been put to sleep I've accomplished a worthwhile goal.

Hopefully, as you read this you will keep an open mind about my suggestions as well. This book is the result of 30 years of focusing on training family dogs specifically. I have personally worked with around 6,000 dogs and their families over those years. My greatest teachers during that time have been the dogs and families I've worked with. Along the way, mistakes were made right along with the successes. I myself am always learning and closely observing what's going on between a client and their dog whenever they interact. I continue to learn from them and on occasion a dog still humbles me. This is a good reminder that I still don't know it all, even after 30 years.

So this book is about training you on how to provide more appropriate leadership within your own family pack, be it one dog or five dogs. The more dogs you have, the more important it is to be a clear leader. Unfortunately, sometimes this goes directly against what you may want to do. Being an appropriate leader within a larger group of dogs sometimes means being less affectionate or doling out your affection in a more controlled manner. If you are the type of person who is constantly going goo goo, gaa gaa over your dogs, you might be undermining your efforts at being the leader. If you are having huge problems with your dog pack and can't control this aspect of your personality, you may need to consider reducing the pack size in order to gain control.

In addition to learning about how to be more appropriate in your leadership, you will learn a way of communicating that creates a highly reliable response from your dogs even in the face of huge distractions. You'll also learn the basics of behavior modification and how to teach your dog to place importance on listening to you. In other words, with a little practice, you will be able to get your dog to place listening to you on the top of their priority list. This may sound hard right now given the level of frustration you might be experiencing, but I can assure you it is not as hard as you might think. So let's get started by giving you a basic education about behavior modification.

Chapter Two

Behavior 101

When I visit a new client for the first time, I give them a basic background about behavior as a foundation to get them thinking on the right track. There are a lot of myths about what works to modify behavior. Behavior modification is just a fancy term for getting a dog (or person) to change something they are doing. If you have taken psychology courses, some of this will sound very familiar. Just think of it as a refresher course on a very elementary level.

To begin, there are two things that will influence behavior. When making reference to behavior, one is referred to as reinforcement and the other is referred to as punishment. Breaking it down further, there is positive reinforcement and negative reinforcement and there is positive punishment and negative punishment. In a moment, I'll give you a simple definition of each one followed by an example of what each one might be. I say "might be" because one of the most common problems I encounter is that a person might think they are doing something to get rid of a problem when actually, they are making matters worse or vice versa, they might think they are reinforcing a behavior when, in reality, they are making their dog less reliable at that command. Let me explain more about this.

First, you need to understand that reinforcement or punishment is not defined by what you are doing to your dog. Rather, it is defined by how your actions affected the behavior you are trying to have an influence on. It is very easy to fall into the trap where you think you are punishing your dog for something it did when in reality you are reinforcing that behavior. This problem exists in both directions. You might also think you are reinforcing something your dog just did, but in reality are punishing the behavior.

Sound confusing? It gets worse. Another related problem may rear its ugly head as well. You may be trying to punish one behavior and as a consequence, you punish something else accidentally that you want your dog to do. Without taking care to look at the whole picture of what you are doing, you might be undermining your efforts. This will become clearer as you keep reading. For now, just be aware that what

23

you think you are doing isn't always being understood by your dog the same way. It's important to look at how your dog is reacting to what you're doing. This will help you in determining whether or not you should continue what you're doing. Someone once said that the definition of insanity is doing the same thing over and over again expecting to get a different result. If you feel like you've been going insane trying to train your dog, maybe you've fallen into this trap.

Here are two examples, where the result desired is not the result achieved. Let's say that Joe Dog Owner has a dog that barks excessively when in his yard. The neighbors are complaining and Joe realizes he needs to do something about it. Joe decides that every time his dog barks he is going to go outside and smack his dog hard on the nose (I do not recommend doing this). But because Joe's dog spends so much time outside alone he quickly figures out that barking gets Joe to come outside more often. As a result, Joe's dog begins to bark more instead of less. Joe thinks he is punishing the barking when in reality he is reinforcing it. The opposite response could have happened in this scenario as well. His dog may have stopped barking and in that case Joe's "cure" would have worked because his dog took Joe's remedy as he intended.

Here's another example on the other side of the fence. Mary Dog Lover has been teaching her dog to come to her when called in her house and yard. She has practiced it a lot and has a very high degree of reliability in that environment. Mary decides to take her dog to the local dog park to let it socialize and practice the "come" command. While at the park, Mary's dog finds some playmates its own age and begins to wrestle with these dogs and is having a grand ol' time. Mary decides to test her dog and calls her dog to come to her. Because she has practiced this a lot, her dog breaks away from playing and comes running over to her. Mary then makes her dog sit and tries to pet her dog. But while she is petting her dog it keeps moving its head in a way that suggests that Mary's dog is annoyed. The whole time she is doing this, her dog is watching the other two dogs playing and doesn't take it's eyes off of them. Most likely, Mary just undermined her efforts to keep her dog coming to her with reliability. Mary should have noticed what she was doing was not rewarding to her dog at that moment. Most likely, it was a mild punishment for coming to her. If she had let her dog go back and play some more she would have used more freedom to socialize and play as a reward. In this case, additional freedom and a chance to play some more would be a much more appropriate reward than petting. However, if Mary's dog had been staring up at her, soaking up her petting with longing eyes, the reward would most likely have been taken as such.

So here are the basic definitions of the two types of reinforcement and the two types of punishments:

Positive Reinforcement: Something pleasant happens to the dog simultaneously or immediately following a behavior that strengthens the behavior and/or makes it more likely for the behavior to occur again in the future.

Negative Reinforcement: Something unpleasant happens to the dog simultaneously with a behavior that strengthens the behavior and/or makes it more likely for the behavior to occur again in the future.

Positive Punishment: Something unpleasant happens to the dog simultaneously or immediately following a behavior that weakens the behavior and/or makes it less likely for the behavior to occur again in the future.

Negative Punishment: Something pleasant or that matters to the dog at that moment is taken away simultaneously or immediately following a behavior that weakens the behavior or makes it less likely for the behavior to happen again in the future.

Don't worry if these don't all make sense yet. You don't

need to be able to recite these definitions. Just understanding the concept of each should help to open new options to you in training your dog to listen. Let me give you some examples of each of these.

Positive reinforcement is something most people are familiar with. An example of positive reinforcement might be giving your dog a treat, petting your dog or throwing their toy for them immediately after they sit, lay down, come or do anything else you might be teaching them to do. There are many things available for you to use as positive reinforcement. Anything you have the ability to provide or deny access to that your dog places value on is a potential reward you can use for positive reinforcement. Things your dog might place a value on could be going on a walk, visiting other dogs or people, being allowed to smell the flowers, being granted permission to chase the resident squirrel up a tree or even being allowed to mark or lift his leg on a tree. One of your first jobs in learning how to get your dog to listen better is to identify what things your dog places value on. It is also helpful to know the basic order they might place them if they could write out a list for you. In other words, rank the rewards in their order of importance to your dog.

Negative reinforcement is something most people are familiar with as well, even if they don't know they are. Most often, negative reinforcement requires the use of some kind of tool in order to apply the negative reinforcement. A common tool most people are familiar with is the bit used in a horse's mouth for training and riding a horse. This tool, when the reins are pulled, applies pressure in the horse's mouth that facilitates getting the horse to respond in the desired way. As soon as the horse does what we want, such as turn or stop, the pressure is removed and the tool returns to a neutral state. Negative reinforcement tools can be very powerful. A horse may weigh a thousand pounds or more and can be easily controlled with this tool. In dog training, there are negative reinforcement tools regularly used to control a dog. One example is the head halter. Some of the common brands are the Gentle Leader and Halti. Head halters control a dog from under their jaw by connecting the head halter to a leash.

To give you a clear picture of how you might use a head halter, imagine you have your dog standing next to you and you have been having trouble getting your dog to sit. To use a head halter ,you would give your command to sit and gently, but firmly, pull straight upward. Your dog's head is going to be pointing towards the sky and if you continue to pull upwards your dog is eventually going to try to get back down to the ground. Since their head and neck is being pulled in an upwardly direction the only thing they can put on the ground is their butt. The moment their butt hits the ground, you release the upward pull and the head halter returns to a neutral, slack position. Many trainers have been quick to employ the use of head halters in their courses. But as is the case with a horse, these tools don't always result in an animal that is responsive when the tool is removed later. Try riding a horse without it's head harness if you're brave and you'll see what I mean.

In my opinion, negative reinforcement tools are limited in their usefulness. In certain situations, such as when you are having difficulty getting your dog to do the desired behavior using any other method or if you're working with a dog that might bite if it feels provoked, they are very useful. In cases like these, the head halter may help you to teach what a command means or might help to keep you safer and in more control. But in my opinion, tools used for negative reinforcement beyond the point where the dog understands what the commands mean are primarily being used as management tools and such will need to be used forever to keep the animal under control in most cases. This is not necessarily a bad thing. Anything that helps control an otherwise uncontrollable dog is better than nothing. Head halters are not, in my opinion, tools that help much in teaching your dog to listen with reliability. In other words, if you use negative reinforcement to try and teach your dog to listen, you will probably find that in the absence of the tool, your dog resorts back to choosing on a case by case basis whether they will listen or not. This is not true with all dogs, but I find it to be true quite often.

I probably just upset a lot of head halter advocates with

that last statement, but I regularly get clients who were trained to teach their dog to walk using a head halter. These same clients tell me that their dog won't walk calmly without it on. If your desired end result is to have your dog listen when they are on or off-leash, then you will probably need to employ other methods and tools to get the job done. Don't get me wrong here. I do occasionally employ the use of head halters in my training for use in situations like the ones I mentioned.

Other tools which can be used for negative reinforcement are choke chain collars, pinch collars, and electronic collars. These tools all can be used in a negative reinforcement manner, but they also have the ability to be used to carry out a positive punishment and are therefore more versatile. Head halters on the other hand cannot be used effectively to deliver a positive punishment without the potential for harm to your dog's neck. You should never yank abruptly on a head halter. You might tweak your dog's neck and give them a whiplash or even permanently injure your dog.

Next we come to positive punishment. Positive punishment, as the definition states, is when something unpleasant happens to the dog that weakens the behavior or makes it less likely to occur again. This is usually the first course of action people take when training or trying to solve a problem or get their dog to listen. If properly used, positive punishment can help in training your dog to listen with a high degree of reliability. But, if not used correctly it can undermine all your efforts. I'll explain more about how to use all four of the reinforcements and punishments later. An example of positive punishment might be squirting your dog with water to stop them from barking at you. If your timing is very good, and the squirt comes immediately following the bark, and if your dog does not like getting squirt in the face, then you have just used positive punishment to weaken the behavior of your dog barking at you. If you continue to use this punishment, you should see the behavior diminish and eventually die out all together. However, if you do this and your timing is bad, your dog may not get the message at all. Or, if you have a dog that thinks its fun to get squirted in the face you would most likely be adding positive reinforcement and strengthening the barking behavior. The old fashioned spanking of a child when they behaved badly is an example of positive punishment.

Finally, we come to negative punishment. Negative punishment is probably the most underused and most misunderstood method to change behavior in a family dog. This could be because most people don't know how to use it or don't know what it is. Negative punishment is very effective in certain situations and completely useless in others. As the definition states, something the dog considers to be of value is taken away simultaneously or immediately following a behavior. This weakens the behavior or makes it less likely to happen in the future. One important point to understand is that the thing you take away needs to be of higher value than the reward your dog receives when they do the behavior. In other words, let's say you have a great treat in your hand and you ask your dog to sit when they are staring intensely at a cat on the lawn a few feet away. If your dog doesn't respond, you could try taking away the treat at that moment. But it will be useless to take the treat away unless your dog places a higher value on the treat than it does on possibly getting to chase the cat.

So what can you take away that is of value to your dog? Well, the first and most obvious thing we can take away is our attention. If you have a dog that jumps on you for attention and you immediately walk away the moment their front paws come off the ground, you would be using negative punishment. The message you would be sending to your dog is that jumping on you results in you taking your attention further away from them than it was immediately before the jump. Negative punishment works through the principle of extinction. Extinction is a term used to describe a behavior dying out because the reinforcement that was present is no longer there. Negative punishment works very well in cases where you are the reinforcement to the behavior.

Other things you can take away from your dog might be their freedom. Here's an example. You have a dog that behaves like a crazy nut when they come into the house. The moment your dog goes wild you take your dog's freedom away by making them lay down and be still for a couple of minutes. When they have shown a little self-control, you give them their freedom back. If they go back to acting crazy, you take their freedom away again. If you repeat this over and over again, you will eventually get the message across that running around crazy results in a loss of freedom and will see your dog slowing down when they are in the house. You can also look at negative punishment from the perspective of taking your dog away from the thing it considers to be of value. Going back to the case of your dog staring at the cat on the lawn, when you ask him to sit and he ignores you, you take him further away from the cat. If he doesn't listen again, you take him even further away from the cat, and so on, until he listens. If you have to remove him from the view of the cat altogether that's what you do. Once he starts to listen again, you can bring him closer to the cat.

The one problem with negative punishment is that it does not always give the clearest message. I believe negative punishment works best when combined with one or more of the other reinforcements and punishments. In fact, that is really true about all of the reinforcements and punishments. If you can find a way to incorporate all of them in a training lesson, you will see very quick results. I'll give you an example of how this could be done in a situation where your dog jumps up on you to get you to pay attention to them.

Let's say you have just walked through your front door and your dog is running up to you to greet you. What you would like them to do is to greet you politely with a sit so you can say "hi" and pet them without them messing up your clothes. But instead of coming to you and sitting politely, they jump on you. What you could do is slip your hand under their collar (the type of collar doesn't matter) and immediately pull them upward and off of you. By pulling upward to a point where you can tell that they are uncomfortable, you have just used a positive punishment for jumping on you. You would then continue to hold their front paws off the ground an inch or so until you see them trying to sit. The entire time you are doing this, their back paws remain on the ground. You are not trying to hang the dog here. This might take a few seconds or even a minute the first time or two that you try it, but stay with it. By continuing to hold their front paws up until they decide to try and get back to the ground you would be using negative reinforcement to teach your dog to sit when they greet you. As soon as your dog is trying to sit, you will set their front paws down, but not until their butt goes down first. As soon as you set their front paws down, you start petting them gently on their head and ears. This is positive reinforcement for sitting. You would continue to pet them until they stand up again which is usually very quickly the first couple of times you do this. The moment they stand up you take your hands off of them. This is negative punishment. You are

34

removing your attention (petting) the moment they stop sitting. If your dog jumps on you again, repeat this every time until they begin greeting you with a sit. Amazingly, you usually only have to repeat this a few times before your dog starts to greet you by sitting first.

So there you have it, an example of how to use all of the reinforcements and punishments together. When you do this you will see there is a synergy not present when you focus on just using one reinforcement or punishment alone. It will take some practice and you may have to think a little to come up with ways to use them all, but the results you see will be amazing provided you are accurately assessing the way your dog is reacting to what you do.

The last thing you should know about punishments and reinforcements is that they are different in the way they need to be applied in order to be effective. Here again is a place where people undermine their efforts much of the time. You'll understand why in a moment.

Behavior research has generally concluded that positive reinforcement when applied in a manner that is variable and intermittent can actually be addictive. The main reason people become addicted to gambling is because the rewards in gambling are variable and intermittent. Variable refers to the reward itself changing in value. The reward could be small or the reward could be a huge jackpot. Intermittent refers to the frequency the reward is received. The person or dog doesn't know when the next reward will come. The combination of variable and intermittent reinforcement is powerful and when applied correctly can work well to strengthen a behavior.

The opposite is true about punishments. In order for punishments to be most effective, they need to occur with perfect consistency. This is especially true about behaviors that have been rewarded for an extended time. I am not talking about first time experiences here. I'll get to that later. What I'm talking about are behaviors that have been in place for a while. Understand first that if a behavior exists, there is reinforcement coming from somewhere. If reinforcement wasn't coming from somewhere, the behavior would not exist.

So if your dog is doing something that it gets pleasure from and you can make it an unpleasurable experience instead of a pleasurable one, the behavior should die out or become extinct. So let's say you have a dog that gets into the trash with regularity and you've had it up to your eyeballs with cleaning up the mess every time you come home. The first step in solving a problem like this is to realize the importance of consistency in applying the punishment you've decided on (I'll discuss various punishments and reinforcements later). Let's say you are a little slack in catching your dog when they are getting into the trash and you only catch them an average of 4 out of 5 times. What ends up happening is that your dog gets rewarded 1 out of 5 times and that reward becomes variable and intermittent. This is a great way to addict your dog to trying to get into the trash. Well, so much for putting an end to that behavior. Do you see the point?

So it is critical that you control your dog's environment when you are not available to give them the consistent feedback they need to receive in order to get them to leave the trash alone. Other factors can enter into this picture as well. Dogs can easily figure out that when you are present, they need to leave things alone and that when you leave, they can get into those things without consequence. This is basically an issue of who owns it. In the dog world, he who has possession of the object is the current owner. If your dog is one that decides to get into the trash only when you are not around, you have not made the message clear that the trash can is always yours, even in your absence. Coming back hours later and scolding your dog when they have already gotten into the trash hours before makes little sense to them. If they are not in immediate possession or in the immediate vicinity of the object you are only going to make your dog leery of you. Giving your dog access to doing the things you don't want them doing when you are not around will only serve to undermine your efforts. There are simple ways to booby-trap your dog so they learn not to do these things in your absence as well. I'll talk more about that later.

I am all for keeping things simple. So, when working with my clients, I break the four reinforcements and punishments down into two categories. I call them positive consequences and negative consequences. Later, I'll show you how to apply consequences in a very specific way that facilitates teaching your dog that listening to you should be at the top of their priority list. But before we do that, I think it is important for you to learn about nature and its influence on learning.

Chapter Three

The Porcupine Principle

Several years ago I attended a seminar given by Gary Wilkes. Gary is a renowned clicker training expert being one of the pioneers in using clickers to train dogs. This seminar was filled with insights and I would recommend attending one of Gary's seminars if you have the opportunity. During the seminar, Gary spoke about how nature has set up the learning process for virtually every living creature on the planet. Gary said, "Nature favors learning through avoidance." This is something that I have been teaching to my clients for years using an analogy I call, "The Porcupine Principle."

Imagine, if you will, a young wolf or coyote in the wild that stumbles upon its first porcupine. Curiosity brings the pup in for a closer look and when it gets just a little too close… BAM. The pup gets a few quills in its nose and runs off yelping. It's a lesson that will be remembered for a long time into the future. What Gary meant when he said that nature favors learning through avoidance is that we remember things that happen to us better and with more clarity when the experience hurts, is traumatizing, or has shock value. These lessons imprint on our brain in one instance. This is quite different from the way positive experiences register on our brain. Positive experiences need a large number of repetitions in order to leave an imprint we can count on. Comparatively, where it may only take one negative experience to have a lasting, long-term memory of an event in our life, it may take 500 or more occurrences of a positive experience to have the same lasting, long-term memory that we can count on from a training stand point.

Think about your own lessons in life where something you did ended up with an outcome where you got hurt or injured in the process. Most people will be reluctant to repeat what they did a second time or at the very least, be more careful and reserved from then on. Can you imagine what it would be like if you jumped off a bridge and broke your foot and you didn't remember the incident eight weeks later. You would be bound to repeat the whole thing again and again and again. Avoidance learning keeps animals and us alive. This is a simple fact. To ignore this element of learning is to become unbalanced. So rather than ignore the power of learning through avoidance we should embrace it and learn how to safely use it effectively in training our dogs.

The trick here is to figure out a way to get a message across that is clear to your dog and at the same time, safe. This is not as easy as it may sound. It is very easy to send a message that is different than the one you want to send if you don't plan your set up carefully. If we examine the Porcupine scenario above, there are several elements you need to be aware of. First, you need to understand that the pup had what I would call "tunnel vision" at the time the porcupine delivered the quills into the pup's nose. There was no mistaking that it was the porcupine who sent the message. Second, the quills going into the nose contains a very strong message of hurt and/or high shock value. And third, it was probably a first time encounter.

You may not be able to have the third element in your message if your dog has a history of doing something that has had benefit in the past. You can however set up a learning situation with at least the first two elements. If by chance you have a new puppy, you have the ability of setting up a situation so the first attempt ends like a porcupine encounter. Doing this before you have a problem will save you tons of frustration down the road. For example, once your dog has figured out that the food you have sitting on the counter tastes and smells better than the food you've been putting in their dish, it is not so easy to get them to leave it alone. So teach them to leave it alone before they have ever gotten a chance to find out how good it is. If you're like most people reading this book, it's probably too late to do this, but keep reading, you'll find out how to solve problems like these even if you have a dog that has been getting away with it for a long time.

How popular would gambling in Vegas be if everyone who went there had to bet everything they brought on their very first bet and lost it all. By setting up a booby trap that teaches them the food they smell on the table is not a good choice, you are essentially doing the same thing. Booby traps should be safe and yet they have to contain a potent consequence to work. Booby traps can even help you achieve a higher status in your dog's eyes. I'll talk more about booby traps later.

Getting back to learning through avoidance, let's compare the lessons you learn through avoidance with lessons that are learned through a positive association method instead. Trainers that teach positive only methods will approach a problem like stealing food off the counter in several ways. They might tell their client to reward everything their dog does that is not stealing food off the counter; this will have marginal success. They might tell their client to ignore their dog every time they jump on the counter; this will have no success. They might tell their client to never put food on the counter or leave

42

the dog alone in the room where the food is at the same time; this will work every time but you haven't really trained the dog. They might tell their client to reward jumping on the counter and put the behavior on command, and then never give the command; this will probably have no success as well. There might be other things they suggest but the messages being sent to the dog, in all of these cases, are not very clear.

Doesn't it make more sense to set up a way for your dog to learn the lesson that food on the counter is unsafe to touch and food in their dish is always safe to touch? This question brings up a very important concept you should understand about the way dogs learn. In her book *The Culture Clash*, Jean Donaldson talks about converting our language from "right vs. wrong" to "safe vs. dangerous" when speaking about a dog's way of learning. Any trainer who has been in the business for very long has heard a client or potential client say, "I can tell that he knows he did wrong because when I come home from work, he acts guilty; and then when I look around, I'll find a pillow he chewed." The scenario may have a different ending than chewing on a pillow, but the number of times I've heard a sentence start like that is more than a thousand. There are two things about this comment that are important. Let's look at them both.

As Jean Donaldson mentioned in her book, we can easily mess up the message we want to send to our dog if we don't set up the lesson carefully. A dog that is left alone with access to items we don't want them to touch can easily learn a message that it is safe to chew these things in our absence, but not in our presence. This kind of thing happens every day. Dogs don't have the ability to understand the concept of right and wrong. It is simply beyond them, and besides, the concept of right and wrong is highly subjective. It is really a matter of opinion. What they do understand is that this is safe to do and this is not safe to do. But dogs can also learn versions of this theme. For instance, your dog can learn it is safe to go to the bathroom in the formal dining room when nobody is around, and it is dangerous to go to the bathroom there when somebody is present. The same goes for chewing; safe in your absence, dangerous in your presence. So it is important to set things up in a way that will not teach them safe in your absence and dangerous only in your presence.

Going back to the Porcupine Principle here. Let's say you come through your front door and see that your dog has chewed on something. You now decide that you are going to punish your dog to teach them that chewing on pillows is wrong (dangerous). So you drag them back to the pillow parts on the floor and do something unpleasant to them. If you analyze this scenario, you will find in reference to the pillow, none of the three elements are present that were present in the Porcupine Principle. Your dog does not have tunnel vision about the pillow at that moment. Second, there is not a potent consequence coming at the moment your dog first touches the pillow, and third, your dog has probably chewed on other things (maybe even pillows or pillow-like things) in the past, so it's not a first time encounter.

Let's look at what really got associated here. You find a pillow chewed and you grab your dog and drag it back to the spot. At this moment, your dog does have tunnel vision…on you. Secondly, a potent consequence is delivered to your dog…from you. And third, this is the first time you found your dog having chewed on something after you walked through the front door coming home from work. This is a first time experience…with you. So what you now have is a dog that reacts to you walking through the front door. The next day, you come home and your dog "acts guilty" when you walk through the door and of course, since she acts guilty you search around and find something else your dog chewed on while you were gone. You repeat the punishment again like you did the day before and only further confirm to your dog that when you walk through the door, trouble is coming… making your dog act even guiltier with each new day you do this. You have now started a vicious cycle which will undermine your efforts to build a trusting relationship with your dog.

A message has gotten through to your dog, just not the message that you wanted to get through to him. Walking through your front door now predicts something unpleasant will happen.

Here's another example of this in action that just recently happened with one of my clients. My clients, a husband and his wife, have a 5 1/2-month-old Boston Terrier puppy. These clients have not exposed their dog to many things up to this point due to the recommendation of her vet. The risks of taking her puppy out before all of the shots have been given are obvious, but in my opinion, socialization is equally important and I'll talk more about this later.

Unfortunately, 5 months is a little late to start socializing a puppy so this puppy was a little nervous at first when it was taken out of the house to new places. Having taken the puppy out about 20 times in their car to fun places, their dog was beginning to lighten up and have fun. When they would get to the dog park, their puppy was anxious to get out of the car to play with the other puppies. The last time they took the puppy out in the wife's car was to the vet to be spayed. My client met me 10 days later at the local dog park where she has been several times before the trip to the vet. Her dog had a great time playing with other puppies her age at this park and was usually anxious to get out of the car. However, this time when she arrived at the park, her puppy did not want to get out of the car. My client told me that she had quite a hard time getting her puppy into the car to come and meet me. Up until the trip to the vet to get spayed, she had never had a problem getting her dog to jump into her car. One trip to the vet for a surgery imprinted on her and she was not about to go through that again. My client then informed me that the dog only reacts this way when it goes out in her car, not the husbands car. This same puppy will jump readily in and out of the husband's car without any problem whatsoever. The wife's car now predicts an awful thing is about to happen. Hopefully, with a little work and a lot of fun trips that association will change so her car no longer predicts something bad is going to happen again.

I tell you this story because it illustrates very clearly how easily a dog learns through avoidance. Having a greater number of trips to fun places first would have minimized the effects of that car ride, but even that may not have assured avoiding the situation. This is really the case in any situation. In reference to training situations where your dog may get the wrong message about something being unsafe only in your presence, try to make a lot of associations that the behavior is safe in your presence when done in the right location (housebreaking) or with the right object (chewing). This will minimize or eliminate altogether the potential for an incorrect association.

Chapter Four

Selective Listening Or Nature's Design?

Let's take a look at nature and it's influence on learning. To begin with, I want to talk about the five different ways a dog has to interpret the world. A healthy dog is born with the same five senses that a human is born with: sight, smell, hearing, taste and touch. Even though we have the same five senses, there is a difference between us in terms of the range of ability we have to employ those five senses when compared with a dog. Some of a dog's senses are much more acute than the same sense in a human and the same is true about some of our senses when compared with a dog. For instance, a dog's ability to smell is more than a thousand times that of a person's ability. On the same token, people have a more pronounced sense of taste than dogs do.

So, let's take a look at how nature intended each of a dog's senses to be utilized. This is by no means a complete list of how a dog may use each sense. What I am trying to point out here is the primary use of each sense. My point of why this is important will become apparent later.

First, we will examine a dog's sense of smell. It has been well documented that a dog's ability to smell is so incredibly sensitive that they can detect a single drop of blood diluted in ten gallons of water. Not long ago, I read somewhere about dogs who have detected cancer in people before tests were able to detect the cancer and just recently, I talked with a person to which this actually happened. For years, the U.S. Customs Department has used dogs for detecting drugs and we know that dogs are used to find bombs in buildings and stadiums. People have speculated about all of the data a dog is able to pick up from smelling another dog or another dog's stool. In a natural setting, their sense of smell is certainly used to help locate and track game, detect dangers, find a suitable mate for breeding, identify familiar pack members, etc. Their sense of smell probably even has abilities that far exceed those I've mentioned. Since we'll never have a dog that can speak English, we may never know the extent of a dog's sense of smell. A dog's sense of smell is so powerful that it's probably safe to say it is the number one sense a dog uses to interpret the world.

Next, we come to a dog's sense of sight. I believe a dog's sight is used for many of the same things their nose is used for such as locating food, identifying familiar pack members, and recognizing potential dangers. Some dogs are very quick to react when they see something that doesn't fit the usual circumstances. For instance, I've heard many clients tell me about times when their dog reacted strongly to them walking into their house carrying something with a strange shape. If the profile of something they consider normal changes, it can move even a normally very calm dog into a state of arousal that suggests uneasiness or even defense. This is why confident dogs are so likely to bite a pool man or construction worker that comes onto your property carrying hoses and poles or has things hanging off of their belt. You should always be careful about circumstances like these; they can be an accident waiting to happen, even with an otherwise well adjusted dog.

With repetition, a dog can get accustomed to seeing these things and become less and less reactive over time. But most of the time, this is a difficult behavior to correct because the dog does not get enough exposure in a concentrated time frame for a change to take place. Have you ever heard of a dog that barks at anything new, like a potted plant or sculpture you set down in the house? This is very common. Dogs are very good at noticing when something has changed and for some

50

dogs, change can be very upsetting. It is also important to note that dogs are very routine oriented. When a routine changes, it can be very upsetting to some dogs to say the least.

When dogs are communicating with each other, there are a tremendous number of body language signals they use. Many of these signals are used for calming other dogs so they know there is no threat. Body language is extremely important if you want to learn how to control your dog better. It is also important to note that dogs learn commands faster or more accurately if the command is taught using a visual signal as opposed to a verbal signal. Patricia McConnell, Ph.D. has talked about a test where puppies from a variety of litters and of differing breeds were taught a simple command. The command was first taught using both the visual and the auditory cue together using a positive reinforcement until the puppies were all getting it correct. She then eliminated one of the two cues. When the visual cue was removed, a large percentage of the puppies did not perform the behavior correctly. On the other hand, when the auditory cue was removed and the puppies were left with only the visual cue, the results were different. The behavior was performed with a much higher degree of accuracy although it still wasn't 100%. This suggests that dogs are more inclined to respond to visual cues than to auditory cues.

I am not saying that your dog cannot learn to pay attention to your voice. What I am saying is dogs seem to have a preferential order to the use of their nose, eyes, and ears. In terms of its universal use, I believe a dog's eyes are second to their nose in how they interpret the world around them.

Next we come to the sense of touch. Touch is something I believe evolution has geared a dog to use for communication, detecting the immediate presence of danger and establishment of status. Dogs in general enjoy being touched. However, there are places on a dog where they are less inclined to let themselves be touched. Some places, such as the top of the head and on their shoulders, are more sensitive to touching. With many dogs, touching them in these places will cause a reaction. Sometimes the reaction can be quite strong. I once lived with a standard poodle that would not let any stranger pet him on the top of his head. If they wanted to pet him under the chin, he had no problem with it. Many dogs will not let their feet be touched. This might be due to improper nail trimming or some event in the past where their feet were hurt.

Over the years, I have seen the behavior of resisting being touched on the head with many dogs. This has led me to conclude that the top of the head, neck and shoulders are a place where touching in these areas carries a message of status. If you touch a dog here, you are saying to them that you are of higher status even when you are petting them affectionately. Watch puppies play and you'll see them stick their head over each other's back directly on top of the shoulder area. Some dogs have no problem with this but others will jump out from under the other dog or even turn around and warn them with a sharp growl and a show of their teeth that they will not tolerate it. Most of the time when a dog tolerates this behavior from another dog, it quickly turns from putting a head over their back to mounting the other dog. This is another behavior that establishes rank and status. Generally, this is all in good fun when dogs play, but this behavior in older dogs will sometimes result in a fight if the dog trying to pull rank doesn't back off from the other dog when told to. I've seen it more times than I can count. If you have a dog that resists being touched on top of the head area, I would suggest you gradually get him used to being touched there. If he doesn't want you to pet him there but lets you touch him in other areas, start in the other areas and gradually move towards the top of the head and shoulder area. Eventually, you should be able to reach out and pet your dog in those spots without him resisting. If you have a dog that acts aggressive when you try to touch him there, I would recommend you find some professional help immediately. On the flip side, touching your dog under the chin area may actually suggest to the dog that you are kissing up to them. This is an area where lower status dogs often go to "kiss-up" to a dog they recognize as higher status. Obviously, we want our dogs to view us as higher status, so by petting your own dogs under their chin you would be sending them a message contrary to this. I recommend that you get used to petting your own dog on top of their head and back area, and refrain from petting them under their chin area. And if they don't like being petted there, don't pet them at all. As you begin to establish yourself as your dog's leader, you will find that this will change and your dog will begin to let you pet him there.

Most social animals do a certain amount of grooming of each other. In most species, the lower status animals groom the higher status animals. I'm not so sure this is true in dogs. I have seen higher status dogs grooming other dogs they are familiar with time and time again. With dogs, it seems to be a behavior they swap with each other. It would be interesting to know whether or not there is an underlying message here. Maybe someone will conduct a controlled test someday where the data can be compiled and then studied.

I believe the sense of touch is also used as a last alert to the presence of danger. I believe this is why dogs that are sleeping will many times react defensively if they are awakened by something touching them. Sometimes dogs that are perfectly trustworthy when they are awake, need to be awakened by making a sound first. One of my own dogs was like this. She wouldn't harm a fly and you could do just about anything to her and she wouldn't react in any way that I would call risky, but if touched while sleeping and awakened, her reactions were not predictable. Possibly, dogs dream and depending on what they are dreaming, they may wake up differently. This is certainly true of people.

The sense of touch is very useful in teaching and training. Rewarding your dog with physical praise is a great way to reinforce a behavior. Very few dogs dislike a good neck or shoulder massage. Properly timed petting can go a long way towards building a solid response from your dog. However, it is also a great way to undermine your efforts as well. Very often I find clients wishing their dog wouldn't be so hyperactive and they try to calm their dog by petting it. They'll be saying something like, "It's okay, it's okay" or "settle down" while they are petting their dog. What they are saying with words and what they are doing with their hands are conflicting messages. Their body language is telling the dog that being hyperactive is worthwhile. After all, it is being rewarded. At the same time they are verbally trying to get their dog to slow down.

Obviously, these are conflicting messages. Petting your dog at this time will only make the dog more hyperactive, not less. In fact, if you take it a step further, these people usually stop petting the dog quickly after it has calmed down which is negative punishment for being calm and finally doing what the people were trying to get their dog to do in the first place. Does this sound familiar to you?

Going back to extinction for a moment, if there is no reinforcement, a behavior dies out. In the above situation, the people will eventually end up with a dog that only rests when they are not around and is active whenever they are around. A conscious effort must be made to go over and reward your dog in some way whenever you catch them calm. Even if it only happens rarely at first, the calm behavior will start to grow in frequency and the hyperactive behavior will begin to decrease in frequency as this behavior becomes the behavior that is ignored. This is not always so easy. As you approach the dog, it will most likely get up again. At this exact moment you must turn sharply and leave in the beginning. Once your dog will let you approach without jumping up, progress will be faster paced.

Reinforcement of inappropriate behavior happens all the time. It is especially common among people that adopt a rescue dog that comes with baggage. As I have already mentioned, dogs that are difficult in social settings are very hard to turn around if socialization began late. To make matters worse, when these dogs are out in public and are having a hard time adjusting to their surroundings, they will usually be reacting in some way that the owner disapproves of and wants to change. The dog might be shaking as if it is scared to death or barking like crazy to ward off the approaching evil demon pushing the baby stroller. Any consoling you might attempt when your dog is acting this way only serves to worsen the problem behavior. If you are going to use praise in a situation like this, you will need to start and stop quickly, like a light switch

56

going on and off, as your dog shows little glimmers of confident behavior. You will need to pay close attention to your dog's behavior so you are only petting or rewarding your dog when it has stepped out of its comfort zone. Petting should cease the moment your dog begins acting the "wrong" way again. Placing yourself at a distance where your dog feels safe from the evil demon pushing the baby stroller is a good way not to put too much pressure on your already flustered dog.

Many trainers prefer positive only methods to teach their clients how to change an inappropriate behavior linked to "bad feelings". These trainers believe that in situations, such as an approaching baby stroller, you should address the problem by working to change the way the dog feels about the thing they distrust or are wary of. They do this through a behavior modification technique called "classical conditioning". An example might be as follows: Using a dog that is paranoid of baby strollers as an example, you would bring your dog to a place where people are known to gather and walk with baby strollers. Placing yourself and your dog at a distance far enough away from the baby strollers where your dog's reaction is minimal, you would begin to give your dog rewards while in the presence of approaching baby strollers. When the baby strollers are not visible, the treats would disappear. Over a period of time, your dog will begin to view approaching baby strollers as a good thing because treats always appear when the baby strollers appear.

By associating good things happening in the presence of baby strollers, you could eventually change the way the dog feels about baby strollers and reduce the reactionary behavior. Over time, you would position yourself closer and closer to the baby strollers, always remaining at a distance that keeps your dog's reactions to a minimum and always at a distance that your dog considers safe enough to accept the treats you are presenting. This in turn will bring about a change in the dog's behavior.

Other trainers will say you can change the way the dog feels about baby strollers by changing the way the dog behaves around them, punishing any inappropriate behavior and rewarding appropriate behavior. When working with this approach, you would give the dog a job to do, such as a sit or down stay. As the baby stroller approaches, your dog will most likely break the stay command at some point when the stroller becomes a big enough perceived threat. When this happens, you would "correct" or punish your dog for moving. As your dog learns that paying attention to you is more important than "worrying" about the approaching baby stroller, your dog's feelings about the baby stroller will change. In essence, you are actually being an example for your dog. You, yourself, are behaving in a way which suggests the baby stroller is of no importance and ignore it approaching. In doing so, you will change the feelings the dog has at the same time. I believe they are both correct because I have seen them both work.

The problem with the first approach is it may take a long time to get results. In my experience, most people will not have the time available to them, or will not be willing to commit the time it takes, to get good results using this approach by itself.

The problem with the second approach is dog owners without prior training experience may not have the expert timing required to appropriately deliver positive and negative consequences to avoid an incorrect association. Also, they may not have the ability to read their dog's behavior correctly and know when it is time to provide a consequence. In either case, I believe this is a situation where some professional help is a good idea. I seem to have gotten off on a tangent here so let's return to the subject of touch.

In my experience, a combination of the two approaches delivers the best and most permanent change the quickest. Beginning with classical conditioning for a period of time until your dog is willing to take the treats in the presence of the stimulus coming reasonably close (this distance may be different for each dog and problem), and then working through operant conditioning after laying down that foundation for a week or two everyday.

I had a client that was having a bit of trouble getting his 6-year-old Golden Retriever to listen to him. I asked him to have his dog lie down on command as a small test. The man knelt down next to his dog and with one hand he pointed to the ground while the other hand was resting on his dog's back. He told his dog to lie down and as he said the words, he started to pet his dog on the back. His dog didn't move a muscle. I pointed out what he was doing and had him take his hand off of the dog. He told his dog to lie down again and his dog did what he asked. His dog was one of the best-trained dogs I have seen in a family home, but there were so many inconsistencies in the communication between him and his dog that he wasn't listening much of time. This was not a training problem, it was a communication problem that stemmed from inconsistency between the different ways we have to communicate and, as usual, the dog was paying attention to the more powerful of the two messages. Body language will always trump verbal language. From the dog's perspective, he was doing the right thing; after all, he was getting petted.

I remember a seminar where a person talked about the power of body language over verbal language. They said that people who are given a visual answer along with a conflicting verbal answer will later remember the visual answer and not the verbal answer. For instance, nodding your head in a "YES" motion while you say the word "NO" will later be remembered as "YES". I doubt this happens 100% of the time, but I would bet it happens more than half of the time.

Next, we come to the dog's sense of taste. Dogs have a lot less taste buds than we do. Their sense of taste is probably the least used sense they have in terms of its universal usefulness. Dogs do like things that taste good and treats are something we can use with effectiveness in our training program. There is a trick to using taste successfully. First, understand its limits. A lot of dogs, once they have a full stomach, will not want even a great treat. It also might not always be available. Second, realize that the timing of when a treat is given is very important and third, how often and when it is given is vitally important. If you are trying to use a more positive approach, it is imperative you get this down correctly. There are two parts to giving a treat. First, there is marking the behavior in some way the moment it happens. This can be the pairing of the behavior with a sound, like a clicker, or a stimulation the dog feels, like a collar that vibrates. The other senses are not of much use for the purpose of marking the behavior. The eyes are not much use because the dog may be looking another direction. The nose because it is difficult to create a smell repetitively and because of the delay that would occur if we tried. This is also the problem with taste and is one of the reasons we use a marker in the first place… it's difficult to give the treat the exact moment the behavior occurs. There is a time delay. The second part to giving a treat is that the moment the dog is getting the treat, it needs to be behaving then as well.

The dog will learn that the reward is for doing the first behavior where the mark occurred but also learns that a certain amount of self control, determined by you, is necessary to receive the treat even after it has been earned.

The most common marker tool in use today is a clicker. This is like a kid's old cricket toy that makes a loud, sharp click. Some trainers have also used an electronic beep noise as a marker. I have used a stimulation the dog feels as a marker, the sensation is exactly like the vibration of a pager going off. We could also use our voice as a marker. When we say "good boy" to our dog we are marking a behavior and when we say "NO" or "bad dog" the moment a behavior we don't like occurs, we are using a marker to mark the bad behavior. You can mark good behavior as well as bad behavior, just be sure you are using a different marker for each one. Later, I'll explain more about markers and their importance in getting a dog to listen with reliability.

Lastly, we come to the dog's sense of hearing. I saved this for last because the subject of the book is why doesn't your dog listen to you even though he understands what you want from him. What I am about to tell you just might be the primary reason that dogs have a strong tendency to ignore commands even after they have been trained. I believe a dog's sense of hearing falls into third or fourth place in terms of its universal usefulness to a dog in interpreting the world. For a moment, let's look at what hearing does for a dog in the wild. First. it may help them locate an animal for a meal, but I believe the sense of smell and sight is more important here. Hearing can also be used to hear the communication of another dog although much of what we've learned about dogs suggests that a lot of their communication is visual body language rather than communication that is heard. Perhaps this is because a dog in the wild would need to sneak up on their prey and be as quiet as possible. Thus through evolution, they learned to communicate more and more with their body over the span of thousands of years because staying quiet helped them to get what they needed.

There are probably other uses for hearing as well, but I believe nature intended a dog's ears to be used primarily to alert them to dangers that they couldn't see or smell first. There are several reasons I believe this to be true. One of the primary reasons I say this is because of the way a dog quickly becomes habituated to their owner yelling "NO" when nothing ever happens afterwards. Habituation is what happens when you get accustomed to something happening that at first caused a reaction. If you moved in next to a freeway, you would probably be bothered for a period of time but eventually you would no longer notice the sound of cars until someone points it out one day by saying, "How can you stand the sound of those cars." Eventually you don't notice the sound. This is habituation.

Dogs quickly become habituated to our voice and the things we say. This explains why a puppy reacts so intensely the first week home when you yell "NO" but by week two is ignoring the loudest "NO" you can muster up. If I'm correct that nature appropriated hearing for the primary purpose of alerting to danger, it would make perfect sense why a dog habituates so quickly to sounds like us yelling "NO" when young. The pup learns that it can dismiss that sound because nothing happens, there is no danger present. I am not saying here that a dog can't learn to use their hearing to notice things that predict pleasant things and thus learn to pay attention to those sounds as well. It was the famous "Pavlov's Dog", that if a bell predicted forthcoming food, then a bell alone eventually caused salivation even though no food was presented. Dogs are remarkable at learning that one thing may predict another. Like the doorbell predicting someone coming in that might be good to visit politely or jump on crazily. This is extremely important and I'll talk more about it later.

Another reason I believe nature put hearing as a sense used primarily to detect danger is because after the age of about 5 months, dogs have an increasingly difficult time getting used to sounds they were not introduced to at a younger age. If you wait until your dog is 6 months or older to begin socializing them to the sounds of the city you will see that it is much more difficult for the dog to get used to those sounds than it is for a younger dog. This is actually true for senses of sight and touch as well. But let's move on.

So a clicker is used to teach or strengthen a behavior. The click is always coupled with the moment the behavior occurs, and a treat or something else of high value is presented to the dog immediately thereafter. With a few repetitions, the dog soon learns the importance of paying attention to the click and what is happening at that moment. They quickly discover that the click happens when they sit for example because you are clicking the clicker every time they sit. It doesn't matter if the sit was accidental or on purpose at first. If you pay close attention you'll see the moment the dog gets it and realizes they are making it happen.

Dogs learn to pay attention to whatever aids them in getting what they want or need and to whatever keeps them away from harm or discomfort. Let me say that again. Dogs learn to pay attention to whatever aids them in getting what they want or need and to whatever keeps them away from harm or discomfort. That about sums it up. Dogs learn to pay close attention to those two simple things. Some people may like to think there is more to their listening or other senses than that. If there is, it pales in importance to those two things. Herein lies the big problem in most homes where a disobedient dog or dog that doesn't listen resides... The people never established a way to convey the message of keeping the dog from harm's way through the sound of their voice. A dog that has learned this message is more easily and reliably controlled than a dog who has never learned this lesson. For this exact reason, I don't believe, after more than 30 years of working only with families and their dogs and experimenting with all positive methods of training and methods balancing positive and negative consequences, that training can be effective on a large scale using positive only techniques.

Let me ask you a question, which do you think a dog learns faster, the lesson of whatever aids them in getting what they want or need, or the lesson of whatever keeps them away from harm or discomfort? If you said the lesson that keeps them from harm, you're learning. So even the way their brain works suggests this is an important lesson. If nature believes it is an important lesson, why are so many trainers so quick to remove this lesson from their program? I think it is one of the downfalls of many training programs that this lesson is not taught. I also think it is the primary reason that dogs who know the command, still won't listen much of the time. If a training program doesn't include this aspect of balance in the program, I believe the program is sadly lacking.

There should be a word you teach in your training that predicts a consequence of approaching harm. This word could be "NO" or "STOP" or "OUT" or any other word you want to use. I use the word "NO" with my clients because for most people, it would be the first thing out of their mouth in an emergency situation. When there is no time to think, reflexes kick in. If the client tells me they use "AH AH" because that's the first thing out of their mouth, I let them use "AH AH" or whatever is best for them. Dogs are not learning English; they are learning to pay attention to certain things we say because we make them realize through our interactions with them that certain things we say have positive or negative consequences and are therefore important. Language is not all-positive. It never has been and never will be.

A vital element is missing when the language you teach your dog does not contain the balance present every where in the world around us. By not teaching this balance, you are left in competition with the environment forever. What it boils down to is you have not developed a way to extend responsibility to your dog, so you keep it all to yourself. I wouldn't really call this training as much as managing your dog 100% of the time. If you want your dog to respond the first time you call it every time regardless of what they are doing at the moment. I will teach you how to create a language which fosters that outcome. By using predictors, markers, and consequences correctly, you can teach your dog to respond with a very high to perfect level of reliability to all sorts of things, including your voice, regardless of the distractions of the environment around you both.

Chapter Four

Creating a Language That
Fosters Reliable Listening

So how do you go about creating a language between you and your dog which fosters responsible listening from your dog? Good question. I'm going to explain to you the way I do it with my clients. This is certainly not the only way to do it; it's just the best way I have found because it's simple and it works every time with every dog.

The pattern of language I use with the dogs I train does not fluctuate. The words change from person to person based on what is most natural for them to use. What you need to know first off is that the words you choose to use are not important. What is important is your adherence to always using the same word or command for every individual behavior you teach your dog and to say it the same way every time. I prefer the tone of my speech to be friendly and casual, but direct, as you would speak in conversation telling someone what you need them to do in a friendly manner. The exception is in how you say the negative behavior marker. You should change the tonality of the word you choose for the negative marker to something different than the way you would usually say the word. In other words, the "NO" I say to mark something the dog is doing that I don't like does not sound at all like the "NO" or "know" I say in a sentence when I'm talking in conversation. I say "NO" as a marker with strong intensity, deeper toned, almost guttural and very crisp and sharp. The basic commands like Sit, Stay, Down & Come however, all have a very friendly, happy, but direct tone to them.

The reason I am telling you to use a different sounding "NO", or what ever word it is that you use to mark unwanted behavior, is because you don't want your dog reacting to this word when you are using it in general conversation. We are going to build up a strong reaction to the word you choose. This word is going to communicate imminent danger. This will give you the power to stop your dog from doing anything at any time. The inflections and intensity of the word should be such that it helps you to get across your feelings that you are not happy

69

with what your dog is doing or about to do and there is danger present. Saying the word in this way will eliminate your dog reacting when you use the word in normal conversation.

It's important you know that the sound of your voice won't have an effect on whether or not your dog listens in and of itself. That result will be determined by how well you follow through with consequences for listening and not listening. For example, you could say your negative marker in a sweet sounding voice. If the follow through I am teaching you is present, your dog would learn that the sweet sounding word, when said the way you have been saying it, predicts imminent danger just like the gruff sounding word. But you would have a dog who reacts to that word anytime you say it, possibly even in the middle of a conversational sentence.

Secondly, you should not switch around and use all of the different synonyms that you know mean the same thing. Your dog isn't learning English. In fact, your dog doesn't understand English at all. Just because we know that Down, George Down, Down George, Lie Down, Lie Down George, George Lie Down, George Lay Down, Lay Down & Lay Down George all mean the same thing doesn't mean that your dog does.

Think of it this way. Imagine you are listening to a language like Chinese or something else where you don't understand a single word. The person talking to you is asking you to do something and you are trying hard to understand them. As they try to communicate what they want from you they say different things to you, just like the list of different ways to tell George to lie down. Occasionally, you hear a phrase come out of their mouth that may sound a little familiar, because it is a phrase they said before, but 99% of what they are saying is gibberish to you because you don't understand their language. As you are trying to remember what the phrase means that sounded familiar, they are ranting and raving 10 other ways to say the same thing to you. The familiar phrase you have been trying to learn and remember is lost in all the other words and phrases they keep saying. As they do this, they are getting frustrated just like you are. In their frustration, they start to raise their voice in volume. The raised voice increases the tension of the moment and you are finding it harder and harder to focus on the words they are saying. You may not even recognize the familiar phrase when they say it at this point. A bad situation gets worse and worse.

As people, we have a very bad habit of raising our voice when we are not being understood. It's crazy, but we act like the person or dog will understand loud English better than they understand the normal volume at which we speak. It's frustrating when you cannot get someone to understand you or to do what you want him or her to do. Our natural tendency is to get louder and louder, repeating ourselves, and/or use the synonyms that we know mean the same thing. Often, we act like the dog we are teaching was born understanding perfect English and knows all the different ways you can use words to mean the same the thing. When in reality they are still trying to learn and remember the way you say it most often. In addition, raising your voice usually speeds up behavior, which is probably the opposite of what you are asking of your dog to do such as sit or lie down.

Lately, I've come to question how a dog listens more and more. It is clear that you can teach a dog to look at you when you say their name. Just click and give them a treat every time they turn and look at you when you say their name. What I question is whether or not a dog learns their name and commands as separate words for instance. I don't think they do unless you specifically teach them that way. I believe dogs learn each individual command as a separate phrase or word. For example, let's say we teach a dog that when we say "George" that means for him to look at us. Next, let's say we teach George that when we say "GeorgeDown" together as if they were one word, that this means to lie down. We could then test how the dog listens by separating the command "GeorgeDown" into two separate words with a noticeable beat in between them. In other words, we say "George" and wait until we get the response of George looking at us, and then we say the word "Down" telling George what we want him to do. What you will see virtually every time, is a dog looking at you like they have never heard that command before. And they haven't. The beat between the words throws off the pattern of how we said it when we taught it. I see it all of the time. My customers say George.... Down with the beat and get no response and then say it as one word GeorgeDown and their dog responds. The frustrating thing is that they don't even realize it most of the time when they do it. They eventually get the dog to respond because they eventually say it the way they taught it or the dog finally figures it out.

When giving commands, it is generally considered among trainers to be good dog grammar if we say the name first and then the command. I believe this to be true, but I also think there is more to it than just putting the words in the proper order. I believe it is also very important to keep the beats between the words the same all the time, and to use the same tonality and inflections in your speech every time. By doing so you will make it much easier for the dog to learn the meanings of your commands. This is a very critical part of creating a language that fosters great listening. Let's take a word you are familiar with and show you how it would affect your own listening and understanding if the word was changed. Using the Japanese word "Sianara", we understand what that means. But what if we said the syllables backwards and said "Narasia" . You would have no idea of what the word meant. I use this example because I believe it helps people to understand how a dog probably hears our words. Remember they are not learning English and do not have the ability to rearrange the words in their head to make sense. Or, another example would be listening to someone that speaks English with a Scottish accent. Personally, I can barely recognize a single word a Scotsman says let alone understand the whole sentence. It is one of the most difficult accents I have ever heard. I went to Costa Rica some years ago and visited a town called Limon. In this town, there were people from many countries who had settled there over the last hundred years. Now, I can understand a fair amount of Spanish and I am pretty good at English, but here the language was very confusing. These people spoke a mixture of English words mixed with Spanish words and some occasional native Indian words mixed together in the same sentences. It was very difficult to understand unless you grew up there. Even Costa Ricans have trouble if they come from other parts of the country.

The language we speak to a dog is the totality of our communication. This includes all the visual body language (when the dog is looking at us), the words (predictors) and other sounds we make, the tone of our speech and the pauses or beats we take as they call it in the movie business. All of these things matter in our communication with our dog. The better we get at mastering being in sync and staying consistent with all of the parts, the better our dogs will listen and understand us. But this alone does not create a dog that will take responsibility for listening to your voice every time you say something to them.

We've already discussed the different senses a dog has and how they may affect a dog's listening. Now let's take it a step further. Think about how all those senses work together to recognize and discover predictable patterns in the world they live in. Dogs are masters at learning predictable patterns that matter to them. What matters to them? We already talked about dogs paying attention to things that help them get what they want and need, and things that keep them from getting in harm's way. These are the things that matter to them. The patterns I'm talking about can be very simple such as the sound of the treat jar opening up predicts a goodie coming their way. They are also capable of recognizing more complicated patterns that are chains of events. I had a client a while back that went to the local dog park with me to do some training. When I work with a client at the dog park, I tell my client to wait for me to give them a cue to when I want them to call their dog. I always say, "OK, call your dog now." I want them to wait for my cue because I want them to call their dog at a certain time when it is distracted by something that might cause it to hesitate or delay it's response. After I give them the cue, they say the command that they have been using to call their dog. After a few repetitions of this, their dog started to come every time I said, "OK, call your dog now." Even though I said this very soft to them, their dog

75

started to recognize the order of things happening. I was quite astonished when I saw how fast their dog had figured out the chain. They didn't even have the time to say the command because their dog was already coming to them every time I would say "OK, call your dog now." Their dog had learned that me saying "OK, call your dog now" predicted that they would be called immediately afterwards.

Dogs are capable of learning many of the smallest nuances that are part of a pattern. For instance, a dog can learn that it needs to listen to one person, in particular, every time they give a command and at the same time learn to completely ignore other members of the same family who use the same command. Even if the commands being used are the same, it does not mean a dog will listen to everyone who says the command. This goes back to what I talked about earlier in the book regarding who has earned the respect of the dog and who has implemented consequences in a way that predicts a certain outcome, good and bad.

As an example, let's say your "average" pattern has always been to say the command "sit" three times in succession getting progressively louder each time you say "sit". On the fourth time you say "sit", you then smack your dog on the rear to get them to do it (I don't recommend doing this). Your dog will quickly learn to pay attention to just how loud and frustrated you sound when saying, "sit." Your dog will begin to listen to the third or fourth command where you reach that point in volume and body language intensity that registers in their mind that it is important to pay attention to you because that is the only way to escape the smack on the butt. All of what you do, every bit of it, predicts getting a smack on the butt at a particular time. You give them the smack on the butt because you think your dog is ignoring the "sit" command. They aren't ignoring anything. On the contrary, they are paying close attention to what matters. Things like the volume of your voice and the intensity of your body language.

In another scenario, let's say your spouse or someone else the dog knows always says "sit" one time calmly and when the dog ignores the command they say a strong "NO" and then smack the dog on the butt just like you do (again, I don't recommend doing this). What they will end up with is a dog that listens to their command the first time they say it without having to raise their voice, instead of the third or fourth time like the dog listens to you. The reason is because a calm "Sit" command that is ignored predicts them saying "NO" which always follows with a consequence the dog prefers to avoid, in this case the smack on the butt again. In your case, getting to a certain volume the third or fourth time you repeat the command predicts the same thing. Your dog has just learned to respond accordingly to what they interpret to be important. We are assuming here that the dog in question performs "Sit" when asked if treats or other things of value are present and distractions are not present.

This is an important lesson to understand in several ways. First, you create the language as you go and your dog learns exactly what your language is, even if it isn't the language you wanted them to learn. In other words, the totality of your language will trump any particular single aspect of your language by itself. My point here is to be careful of the pattern you show your dog. They will learn all the little parts of it. This may include the parts you try to hide from them or don't even know you are presenting to them.

In the seminar I attended given by Gary Wilkes, he talked about a man that was training his dog with a clicker. The man said his dog could now read his mind. He believed the dog knew when he was going to receive a treat and when he wasn't going to receive a treat. The man was making up his mind each time before he was giving a command whether or not he would give the treat that time. When he had decided to give a treat, the dog responded every time correctly. When he had decided in his mind that he was not going to give the treat, the dog ignored the command. The man was filmed training his dog. After studying the film for clues of why this was happening, it was noticed that the man put his thumb inside of the clicker hole where he could click when giving a command he intended to treat. When he was giving a command that he intended not to treat, he was keeping his thumb outside of the clicker hole about a 1/4 inch from where it would be if he were going to treat the behavior so that he wouldn't accidentally click the clicker at those times. The dog was sharp enough to notice the positioning of the man's thumb down to only 1/4 inch, and it predicted the outcome of the encounter. How subtle are some of the signs you give to your dog that you don't even know you give?

The second reason that lesson is important is it proves a dog can learn a pattern that predicts the nonoccurrence of an event. Put another way, your dog is capable of learning that in order to avoid getting a smack on the butt, they must pay attention to what you asked them to do and comply. Noncompliance equals the smack on the butt and compliance equals something good happening and avoidance of the unpleasant consequence.

If you want your dog to listen every time, the first time you ask, you need to create a predictable pattern of events that your dog finds important. The first step in all of this is to teach your dog what the words mean that you are going to use to control your dog. My basic class teaches the following words... No, Come, Sit, Down, Heel and Stay. Later, I will explain the importance of each of these commands. In addition, I usually add some fun things like roll over & waving hi.

So, first we train our dog to know what the words mean. But, what about the homes I visit where the dog is not a puppy anymore and the dog knows what the words mean already. I am not going to tell you how to teach your dog the actions of sitting, staying, coming, heeling, and lying down. What I am going to teach you is how to communicate in a way that fosters a high, if not perfect reliability, to listening to you.

There are parts to your dog's training. I am assuming that you've covered the first part and know your dog understands the words when they are in a stimulus free environment and that there is something obviously in it for them such as a treat, petting or play. Now you need to teach your dog to listen to you when you use those words in the face of everything distracting around them.

I call it the "Priority Rearrangement" phase of your dog's training program. I usually begin this part of training with a simple negative punisher of walking away with the treat I have in my hand if the dog doesn't respond or responds incorrectly. If the dog is more interested in something else I would use that as the reward or the non reward and take the dog further away from the object of their interest if they didn't respond and take them closer to the object of their desire if they respond correctly. In other words, I would set up the learning experience for the dog so they get the message that their best chance of getting what they want is by paying attention and responding to whatever I ask them to do. If they don't respond, I would say "NO" and immediately put the treat behind my back or turn and take the dog with me away from the object of their desire or even better yet, both. By starting this way, I introduce the dog to the concept of "NO" having a consequence that means they missed out on something important to them. This only works if the thing you think is important is actually important to them at that moment. Even though this is a minor consequence, to some dogs it is all that might be necessary to get them to respond the next time you give them that same command. Over time, the dog will discover there are other consequences to the word "NO", some of which will be positive punishments, and none of which will be desirable to the dog. In the controlled environment of a training session, I can introduce the word "NO" with all of the importance I want to attach to it. In a moment, I'll show you how you make it even more important. Right now I want to show you why it is so important that your dog knows the importance of "NO" from an avoidance standpoint.

The strongest survival instinct is to stay out of harm's way. It is a fact that people will try harder to avoid an unpleasant situation than they will to attain a pleasantry. This is true for dogs as well. The reason the brain so quickly imprints unpleasant experiences is because unpleasant experiences avoided are generally synonymous with potential harm avoided. This is the easiest message to imprint on our dog's brain but in so many homes, the message has never been taught. Here's why it is so important...it keeps them alive. And it does so in more ways than one. It keeps them alive when we can say "NO" and stops them in their tracks so they don't head into oncoming traffic in the street. It keeps them alive when you can say "Come" and know that they will stop as fast as they can, and turn around and head back to you and away from the dog that looks like it wants to kill yours. But probably most important of all is that it keeps them alive when you have control of them and don't feel like taking your dog to the shelter or pound every 5 minutes. Let's face it, there are many more dogs killed in pounds and shelters due to the owner's lack of control than on the highway. In my opinion, this is probably the most important of all the messages we teach our dogs in training, and any program that doesn't teach this is sadly lacking.

We have brought dogs into our environment to live with us in our homes. Homes that have electrical cords and streets that have cars, etc. In the wild, a dog learns to avoid things that are different than the dangers they might encounter living in our world and they learn those lessons through avoidance, so why is it that so many trainers avoid or neglect to teach this lesson?

Now, let's get on with the business of building our language. I said that dogs are experts at learning patterns. What this really means is that dogs are great at learning predictors. They learn the order of events quickly if they occur the same way repetitively. Like the doorbell ringing and somebody going to answer the door and someone being there outside of the door when it opens. But the actual order of the learning takes place in reverse. In other words, they learn from the end to the beginning. Here is an example of the learning process... Let's say you have a dog that steals tissue out of the trash bin in the bathroom. You quietly watch your dog get up and head to the bathroom. You follow very sneakily and catch her with her head in the bin, a moment of tunnel vision. With a beanbag in your hand you say a loud sharp "NO" and bean your dog on it's butt with the beanbag. The affect of the beanbag bouncing off your dog has the effect of being a hit without injury. It was a lucky break if you will. Your dog survived a close encounter. A beanbag can be made from a small sock and dried beans that you then tie off. The beanbag does not have to be big to be effective. If you have a very small or fragile breed I would not recommend doing this at all. You must use your judgment. If you don't feel comfortable with a small beanbag get a good water pistol or sprayer. Or roll up a towel or wash cloth and put rubber bands around it. If you have a big tough breed you may need to use something stronger yet. The important thing is that something startles your dog through the sense of touch immediately after you say your sharp "NO."

What happens in the "head in the trash can" scenario is that your dog discovers that when they hear "NO" it is followed by a potentially strong consequence. So, the first thing your dog is going to learn from the above is that "NO" has a consequence. If it was the first time he ever tried sticking his head in the trash, you may have even "stopped" the behavior permanently. After you start to apply a consequence every time you say "NO" for something you don't want your dog to do, you will begin to see your dog reacting when you say the sharp "NO." Most likely you now have a dog that stops what it is doing or about to do when you say "NO." This is a critical stage in your dog's learning. It is very important that you continue to apply the consequence even though your dog now reacts when you say "NO." This is a turning point. If you stop applying the consequence which has gotten your dog to react, you will also stop his learning and be stuck in a management mode. You will be able to get your dog to stop doing something but your dog has not taken the final step of accepting responsibility to stop doing those things that cause you to say "NO" in the first place. By continuing to apply the consequences, you will force your dog to see its own pattern of bringing on the chain of events that led to the end consequence. Much like your dog made the connection that when they put their butt on the ground they heard a click and then a treat appeared or something else good happened. They learn that they are responsible for the chain of events that occur.

Here is an example of the learning process using both a positive outcome and a negative outcome... Let's say you are teaching your dog to sit on command and you are using a clicker to mark the behavior of sitting and treats as their reward. It works like this...

Step 1. You click>You give them a treat.

You would repeat Step 1 until your dog has figured out that a click equals a treat.

Step 2. Your dog sits>You click>you give them a treat

You would repeat Step 2 until your dog is throwing sits at you in rapid-fire succession. In other words, you do this until your dog is offering a sit often enough and quickly enough that you can easily anticipate or predict when they will sit next.

Step 3. You give the "sit" command>Your dog sits>You click>You give them a treat.

In Step 3, you start adding the command in front of the behavior happening. The command, be it a single word or phrase, will become the cue that predicts the chain of events that are about to take place. In Step 3, we stop marking and treating the behavior we are teaching whenever the dog offers it to us without being given the command to do it. I recommend that my clients stay at Step 3 until they have done about 500 repetitions over the course of 2 weeks. I do this for 2 reasons. First, I want my clients to get used to saying the command the same way every time so that we can be reasonably sure that their dog has learned the command with all the little variances in how my client might say it. Even though they are trying not to change the way they say it, they still do. And secondly, I want to be reasonably sure that the dog has built more than just a short-term memory to what the words we are teaching actually mean.

Steps 1, 2 and 3 should be done in a location where the distractions are few to none. In Step 4, we begin to add distractions to the learning situation and begin shifting your dog's priorities around so that you will be at the top of the list every time. Step 4 has two possible endings…

Step 4. You give the "sit" command>Your dog sits>You click>You give them a treat.
or…

Step 4. You give the "sit" command> your dog DOESN'T sit>you say "NO" to mark the noncompliance>you walk away with the treat and/or take the dog away from the distraction.

Consider Step 4 to be like an introduction to negative consequences for not listening to a command we have been teaching. I find that training moves along much more quickly if you watch your dog carefully and are able to catch the moment they make the decision to pay attention to the distraction instead of the command. In other words, in the beginning of this step try to give them the command when they are looking at you if possible and then the moment they look away at the distraction say "NO" and take away the treat or take them away from the distraction. If you are taking them away from the distraction you will need to have them on a leash to be able to do this.

Step 5. You give the "sit" command>Your dog sits>You click>You give them an extra special treat or praise them.

or...

Step 5. You give the "sit" command>Your dog doesn't sit>You say "NO" to the noncompliance>You administer a positive punishment consequence of some kind simultaneously or immediately following the word "NO".

In Step 5 we start to raise the level of the consequences for not responding to the command, to one with higher intensity. Step 5 is done with your dog on leash. Positive punishment consequences might be adding a quick jerk on the collar the dog is wearing through the leash for example. Your dog's sensitivity level and your strength and ability will determine the type of collar to be used. In the chapter on tools, I will discuss the various collars available to use and the pros and cons of each one. You should also continue to take your dog further away from the distraction following the positive punishment. Walk a few yards and then repeat Step 5 again. Continue to do this until you get the response from your dog that you are asking for. Once you get your dog to respond to your command give them an extra special treat. But be aware that many times when you begin Step 5, you will see a look of shock on your dog's face. The surprise of the consequence can cause your dog not to accept treats in the beginning. If your dog does not want to accept treats at this time switch to petting your dog. Be extremely loving to your dog at this moment. You want to comfort your dog and reward them when they finally do respond no matter how difficult it was to get them to do the command. This is very important. You want to make sure that your dog considers you to be a safe place to come to any time, not someone to avoid.

Many times a positive punishment will cause a change in your dog's demeanor, most likely having a calming affect. This is a huge opportunity and I want to impress upon you the importance of this. Every time you use a positive punishment after an undesirable behavior occurs, be it not listening to a command you know that your dog understands or stopping your dog from doing something you want to permanently extinguish, you usually have an opportunity that follows immediately after the punishment. That opportunity is to reward the change that is brought about by the punishment. For example, let's say you have a dog you catch grabbing clothing and you say "NO" and immediately throw a beanbag at their butt. Your dog then reacts to this by going and lying down a moment later. This is an opportunity to reinforce the calm, quiet behavior that could eventually take the place of the obnoxious behavior of stealing clothes. You could even give your dog something to chew on that they like that is appropriate for chewing. The point here is not to be lopsided. Punishments open up opportunities. They alone are not the cure and never will be. If punishment alone were the answer, we would not have repeat offenders in our jails. For every punishment, you should attempt to reward the change that occurs due to the punishment. Remember, the scenario I spoke of earlier in the book about using all four punishments and reinforcements to solve a jumping up problem and replace the behavior with sitting politely for a greeting? This is what I'm referring to here. If you don't do this, you may find it takes much longer to stop the problem behavior or get your dog to recognize the value of listening, if "not listening" is the reason you gave the punishment. You may even find that one bad behavior is replaced by another bad one instead of a good one. I want to stress this because in most every home I

89

visit where the people and the dog are in conflict, it stems from a lack of balance. Either the people are not good at delivering a punishment that matters to their dog and they are constantly giving their dog attention and rewards for nothing in particular; or they are not good at rewarding good behavior and are constantly disciplining their dog for the things they do wrong. Many times, this second group of people become overly harsh and abusive in the process of trying to train their dog because they are not paying any attention to the new behavior opportunities that pop up from the punishments. Balance is important. Show your dog what is good to do as well as what is not good to do. This requires making a conscious effort on your part if you fall into one of those two categories and most likely you do if you're reading this book. It is not always easy to do this because it may go against your nature. I will promise you though, that it makes a huge difference to "pay attention" to everything. By "pay attention" I mean to give appropriate and timely feedback to your dog through positive and negative consequences. This will ensure that you are clear in helping your dog to understand what you like them to do as well as what you don't like them doing.

Step 6: You give the "sit" command>Your dog sits>You say "Good Dog">You give them an appropriate reward.

or…

Step 6. You give the "sit" command>Your dog DOESN'T sit>You say "NO" to mark noncompliance>You administer a positive punishment using an off-leash consequence.

Step 6 is conducted with your dog both on a leash and then off of the leash in a safe, fenced environment. Here you will teach your dog to respond every time you give a command regardless of the distractions present, with or without a leash on your dog. The object is to demonstrate to your dog in a safe manner with major impact that ignoring your command can have dangerous consequences. I highly recommend using one of today's modern e-collars for this step. An e-collar allows you to have perfect timing and also to deliver a consequence that is tailored to your own dog's sensitivity across a great distance. Other off leash tools are available but you must have your dog in close proximity to you for most of them to be useful. The most common tool used other than an e-collar is a throw chain. This is similar to the beanbag but has more weight and impact behind it. I personally haven't used a throw chain for a long time. The reason being that modern e-collars are so adjustable to the size and temperment of the dog that it seems a bit archaic to use throw chains anymore. But they do work well when used correctly.

Beginning with your dog on leash, you will wait for an opportunity to give your dog a command when it is clear they will need to make a choice between listening to you and continuing to pay attention to something else. I usually begin with the "Come" command. I start here because I want to teach the dog first and foremost that coming when called is always the safest choice. I want the dog to learn it is never dangerous to come to their owner and that in fact, it is the safest place for them.

It takes about a half a second to know if your dog is going to turn and come to you. If your dog turns to come to you, immediately mark the response verbally with "good boy" or whatever positive marker you are using and continue with the verbal praise until they are all of the way to you. If your dog has turned to look at you and you start saying "good boy", or whatever words you use to encourage him to finish what he started, and he just stands there with out moving you, will say "NO" and push the momentary button on the remote transmitter. If your dog ignores you completely or turns to look at you and then goes back to what they were sniffing, you will press the continuous button on the remote transmitter for about a second. Once your dog is on the way to you again continue to say "good boy" or whatever your words are the entire way back to you.

This continuous feedback is important in the beginning for two reasons. First, because it enables you to show your dog they are on the right track as they complete coming to you and secondly, because it provides a contrast against which you will mark the moment your dog deviates from the course of coming to you. As your dog is on their way back to you they will most likely deviate from the course occasionally in the beginning. As you are saying "Good Boy" all the way back to you, you need to be prepared for the split second your dog loses focus and changes direction to go see or do something else. At the exact moment your dog makes the decision to change course, you will mark that moment by saying "No" and push the continuous button on your remote transmitter at the same time or immediately thereafter. You will hold the button down until your dog stops going in the wrong direction and then release the button. If your dog is already on the way back to you from this consequence, continue to verbally mark your dog's actions until they get to you or until they deviate from course again. If they deviate again, you will repeat the process by saying "No" again and hold down the continuous button until they stop going in the wrong direction or are back on course. If your dog stops going the wrong way but doesn't resume their course towards you, you will repeat the command to come again and start the entire process over. Once your dog gets to you, guide them into a sit position. If you want them to do something else when they get to you, have them finish that way and then praise them or give them a treat reward. At this point I have usually stopped using treats completely due to the rules of the local dog parks not allowing food inside the park. If you do not have this constraint, you can use treats on an intermittent schedule for a while longer if you like. This intermittent schedule should get less often over time. As you reduce the frequency of giving the treats, you will pick only those times that your dog comes to you without using the remote to give them a treat reward.

When first using the remote trainer, watch the reaction your dog has when you press the button. You want the stimulation to have an impact but not one that sends your dog into a screaming maniac or causes your dog to lie down and not want to move. If your dog goes berserk, you have the collar set too high. If your dog lies down and doesn't move, you may have the collar set too low. If your dog lies down and doesn't want to move and you increase the stimulation substantially with no success in getting your dog up and moving, you should connect a long leash to your dog and use the collar in conjunction with the leash to help them get moving. This usually means you did not put in a good foundation of what come means in your on leash training. Some of the e-collars on the market are too strong for certain dogs, but fine for others and vice versa, some of the collars are not strong enough for certain dogs and great for others. I have seen both situations many times.

I have a few rules I follow for at least the first week of

working off leash with a remote training collar. The first rule is that I do not call a dog when they are in a social interaction with another dog or with a person. All situations where I call the dog are away from things other than people or dogs. In the second week of training, I don't call the dog away from people that are petting them but I will call them away from people if they are not being touched. I begin this by making myself look very inviting and nonthreatening by squatting down and being within close proximity to the dog. When it comes to calling the dog away from other dogs, I begin by calling the dog to me when they are not interacting with dogs that I believe to be communicating through their body language that they are of higher status than the dog I am working with. After a few sessions like this, I will call the dog from virtually all situations.

One important lesson that needs to be taught to your dog is that you are always the safest choice. Most dogs will go through a period of testing. They will try to find some place they can go to escape and avoid the stimulation. They may go and position themselves under a desk or chair where they frequently lie or they may go back to a person that was petting them earlier and sit next to them. Where they go is not important. What is important is that you understand your dog doesn't yet understand that there are no consequences if they listen to you. This process you are going through here will ultimately show your dog that you are the safest of any safe place to come to.

All of this is actually very easy for your dog to learn. Nature teaches its lessons in this way, so you are actually working with the natural learning process not against it. As you work with your dog, you will notice that your dog is responding more and more accurately to your command to come. You will find that you are using the e-collar less and less because the mistakes are occurring less often. As this takes place, you should gradually increase the level of the stimulation you are using a little at a time. You do this for two reasons. First, you want the consequence to increase because the opportunities to add consequence are becoming further and further apart. By increasing the stimulation a little at a time you will insure that the reminder is one that makes the next occurrence even further apart than the previous one. The second reason is because your dog may become habituated to the feeling of the stimulation over time. I can use myself as an example here. I currently visit an acupuncturist that hooks me up to a machine that delivers an electrical stimulation between two of the needles. The stimulation is virtually identical to the stimulation of the e-collar used to train your dog. The purpose is to help rehabilitate an injured muscle. When he first hooked me up to this machine the feeling annoyed me, but after a few sessions, I found myself falling asleep with the stimulation going through my shoulder. Granted, the stimulation used to rehabilitate my shoulder is less intense than that needed for some training situations but the fact is that I could fall asleep with this electrical impulse running through me.

Your dog may become habituated to the sensation as well. Increasing the level of the stimulation, as mistakes become less and less frequent, will ensure that your training is heading towards no collar being necessary down the road.

In order to reach a point where no collar is necessary you must build the language between you and your dog in a way that your dog finds what you say always to be important when it pertains to him. The process I have just shown you will do just that. If you change things around and forget to say "No" for instance, or you say "No" after the stimulation has occurred you will not have built a language which allows you to communicate imminent danger to your dog. Remember, your dog has a mind of it's own. It was born with a mind of its own and it will die with a mind of its own. This is something you cannot change. But by creating a language like the one I've shown you here, you will never be in competition with the environment.

Once you have your dog responding well to the "Come" command, you should practice the process with other basic obedience commands. When working on the other commands, I usually use only the momentary button. However, I may use the button in a pulsing manner as I repeat the word "No", pushing the button each time I say "No." I determine this by the response of the dog. For instance if I give the command "Sit"

97

and I see the dog decide to do something else, I will say "No" with a push of the button. If the dog decides to do something else or try what they were about to do instead, again I may repeat the "No" again 2 or 3 times, each with a push of the button. This pulsing of the stimulation in many cases works better than continuous stimulation or raising the level of the stimulation. I cannot tell you what will be better for your personal dog since every dog reacts a little differently. I simply put it out there for you to experiment with this before you immediately decide to raise the level of the stimulation. If you are unsure about what to do here, I would highly recommend hiring a trainer that understands how to use an e-collar properly.

Chapter Six

NILIF

Creating a language between you and your dog that fosters reliable listening is the beginning to having a great dog that listens well, however, there are other factors that come into play when training. These other factors help to eliminate as much of the negative aspects of training as possible. The better you are at implementing these other factors, the more positively based your training will become. One such factor is the NILIF concept.

So what does NILIF stand for? It stands for "Nothing In Life Is Free". This is the first factor you should concentrate on if you are the kind of person who wants to love your dog into listening to you. Let me start by pointing out that every animal on the planet works for their living. That is, every animal except the family dog and cat. Think about it for a moment. Dogs get free room and board, daily massages, special treats and who knows what else depending on the home they are living in. This is unnatural and can lead to problems of varying degrees depending on the overall nature of your dog. Dogs with strong leader qualities may become more and more demanding of their owners, acting like they control the house and that you are nothing more than a slave who resides there to serve them. If you have a dog that has started to act like it is his right to have first choice, your relationship with your dog could benefit from implementing a "nothing in life is free" rule.

Think about it like this... if your dog gets everything he needs and wants, whenever he or she desires it from you without having to do anything to receive it, why should they listen to you when you ask them to do something? If your thinking is along the lines of "he should listen because I'm nice to him" or "he should listen because I always give him whatever he wants", then you are in big trouble. I'm not saying every dog will become a problem if they get everything they need or want for free all of the time. Some dogs will be fine without having to implement the NILIF rule. I do believe though that ALL dogs are happier when they begin to earn their keep just like kids appreciate toys they have earned more than toys that were given to them.

So, how do you begin to implement this rule? First, you need to realize that you are in control of virtually every resource your dog needs or wants. Whether or not your dog gets fed tonight is entirely up to you making their food and giving it to them. Whether or not your dog gets to go on a walk is entirely up to you putting them on their leash and taking them out. There are many other things you are in control of as well and your first step here is to begin to identify what resources you have control over. Opening the back door to your yard is a resource, food is a resource, toys are a resource, preferred resting spots are a resource, access to visiting other people and other dogs are something you control. In fact, access to anything your dog is interested in is something you can control.

Once you have identified the resources you have in your control, and they are many, you need to teach yourself how to ask for something from your dog before they are given these things. Begin with simple things like asking for a sit before you are going to feed them. Gradually, you should increase your demands. And these are demands. You must learn the concept of tough love here. Your dog will not receive what it wants until you get what you have asked for. For instance, if you ask for your dog to lie down so that you can give them their food and they don't lie down, tell them "No" and set their food on the counter out of reach and walk away. Come back in 5 minutes and ask them again. If they give you what you've asked for, give them their food, if not, repeat the process.

The concept is kind of like going to work. Whether you're the boss or you work for someone else, employees get paid after the work week is over. The vast majority of people don't get paid at the beginning of the week for the work they are going to do that week; they get paid at the end of the week. Keep this in mind as you implement this "nothing in life is free" concept.

This may be difficult for some people to do. Most people don't get a dog to become a boss. They get a dog so they can love it. If you are this type of person, you need to see the correlation between the two and understand that they are not exclusive of each other. I had a client a couple years ago WHO wanted to spoil her dog constantly. She asked me the same question over and over and my answer to her was always the same. She wanted to know if her dog was going to resent her if it had to do something first. This woman cooked hamburger for her dog every night and truly loved doing it. In her mind, asking her dog to do something first meant the same thing as not being able to spoil her dog. She knew that her dog was completely obedient to me and loved me to death. She also knew that I always asked her dog for something, verbal or nonverbal, before I would pick her up and cuddle her. She could see that her dog adored me and always commented on it every time I saw them. What I kept telling her was that she could keep on giving her dog everything that she liked to. She did not have to

102

stop giving her dog anything. She simply had to stop giving it away for free. It was not easy for her to do this, but eventually she began to get the hang of it with lots of reminding and practice.

It is not always true however, that you can keep giving your dog everything even when they do something for it first. There are some dogs that need to have certain restrictions placed on them and kept in place for the lifetime of the dog. You could call it a trade off. I personally had a dog that was like this. When I received him, Boscoe was a matted mess that a friend of mine had found in front of a grocery store in Hollywood. It seemed he had no home so my friend brought him to me and asked if I wanted him. I took him in, cleaned him up and nursed him back to good health. Shortly after taking him in, I discovered that he had a terrible marking problem. Boscoe was sneaky though. He never marked anything in front of me. I tried all of the tricks I knew to catch him marking, but only once did he ever attempt to mark in my presence. I soon discovered that Boscoe would only mark when I was away from home. I decided to barricade Boscoe into the room that had his dog door leading outside using a baby gate. Boscoe marked that room once and never marked in that room again. This seemed to solve the problem. After several months, I decided to give Boscoe freedom to roam the rest of the house again. Within a week, the marking began again when I was away from home. I went back to blocking his access to everything except the room with his dog door and everything was fine again.

After about 6 more months I tried again to give him the freedom of the entire house and again the marking returned. Over the 8 1/2 years I had him I tried several more times to give additional freedom to Boscoe but he always went back to marking when I was away from home. Boscoe taught me a good lesson about the importance of controlling space with some dogs. The reason I tell you this story now is because it turned out to be a trade off between him and I. He knew I was the boss when I was home, but in my absence he took over. By controlling his space, I was able to keep the behavior under control for the entire time I had him, other than those times when I was testing him.

Not all dogs will be like Boscoe. Many dogs will be able to be given the freedom of the entire house after a period of time controlling their freedom. But occasionally I run across other dogs that are like him and the owner needs to accept that there is a trade off to keeping their dog from doing certain things. It may not be a marking problem we are talking about. The bottom line is that if the dog has not earned the right to have the resource you would like to give him, you simply can't give it to him until he has earned the right to have it. And some dogs may never earn the right to have it. Boscoe was probably about 5 to 7 years old when I got him. Perhaps if I had received him as a puppy things would have turned out differently.

Chapter Seven

Hidden Messages In Those Basic Commands

Have you ever wondered why the term "basic obedience" even exists or why the same five commands make up the basic obedience list no matter what training class you attend? The reason is simple. With the exception of "Sit", each of the basic commands have a hidden meaning behind them. The four remaining basic commands are "Heel", "Down", "Come" and "Stay". These four commands help to shape how your dog will view you in your relationship as well as make your dog easy to control. The commands help to make you a higher status member of the family pack. The remaining command, "Sit" is what I refer to as a "convenience command", meaning it is simply convenient to have a dog that knows how to sit when told to.

Regardless of how you teach these commands initially, you will eventually get to a point where you will be working with your dog around distractions that pull your dog's attention away from listening to you. When you get to this point in your training, you should begin to apply the balanced approach of implementing negative consequences along with the positive consequences. It is only when you begin to apply balance that you convey the meaning that is hidden in each of the commands. Now, let's take a look at these five basic commands individually and see how they effect your dog's opinion of you.

Heeling

First, let's talk about having your dog heel next to you on a walk. You've probably seen people walking their dogs hundreds if not thousands of times. And you've probably walked your own dog or someone else's dog in the past. More often than not when you see someone walking a dog, it resembles the dog taking the person for a walk, run or even pulling and dragging them down the street. The person is behind the dog, leash extended to its full length and the persons arm outstretched, trying to hold on if it's a large dog.

Heeling your dog refers to having your dog walk next to you on your left or right side with a loose leash and allowing you to lead where the walk will go. The whole concept of heeling is

107

to have your dog let you lead the way. It is a leader and follower exercise/activity. You are either leading your dog or you are following your dog. Obviously, if you want your dog to listen better, you want to be the leader.

Over the last 30 years, I have come to understand the importance of heeling beyond what it appears on the surface. My experience has shown me that for about one third of the dogs I train, this will be the most important exercise we do. There are a lot of dogs that will put up a huge fight to have their way when on a walk. These dogs usually have issues about being led and heeling is the exercise that deals with this directly. For those dogs that have a huge resistance to heeling this may be what I call a "breakthrough exercise". A breakthrough exercise is an exercise which helps dissolve other problems that are seemingly unrelated to the exercise itself. Think of it as the nucleus to the problems when the dog is resisting the exercise and the nucleus to having a well-behaved, obedient dog when they finally comply with the exercise. Heeling with attention also lays down a strong foundation for having good off-leash control of your dog later. Even if you never intend to take your dog on a walk, it is a very useful exercise to do with your dog. The concept of your dog looking at you as the leader in your relationship on a walk will carry over into how your dog looks at you inside the house and in other situations.

I teach heeling by simply doing the opposite of the dog

every time they take the lead on the walk. If the dog moves ahead of me, I do an about-turn in the direction opposite of the side I am walking the dog on. For instance, if I'm walking the dog on my left (the traditional side for heeling), I'll do a 180 degree right about-turn every time the dog moves ahead me. The dog, being in front of me, doesn't notice I have changed directions but quickly finds out that I have when the leash pulls them in the new direction I'm headed. After a few turns most dogs will start to hang back a little bit so they can keep an eye on me and see what I might do next. After each turn, I usually walk about 10 feet and then turn back to go in the direction I was headed before the dog tried to take the lead. This second turn will usually be a turn that has the dog paying extra attention because they were just caught off guard with the first 180 degree turn. It gives the dog the opportunity to see that when they are not paying attention, things don't always go so well and when they do pay attention things go very smoothly. If the dog moves out away from me to my left I'll do a 90 degree right turn. If the dog crowds my left leg, I'll turn directly into them and do a very tight 360 degree left hand circle to get across the message that they need to respect my space even though they are to stay close and keep their attention on me. By making them back off from my leg a little bit, they learn that the only way to always know where I am and to be prepared for what I'll do next is to check in with me by looking in my direction with regularity. This looking to check in with me is one of the most important elements of the process. Once the dog has discovered the importance of checking in and looking in my direction regularly, a habit starts to form that will carry over into how they behave off-leash later.

You may have a dog who tries to "beat the system" and starts to lean on you as you walk instead of look at you. Much of the time, this is because your dog has figured out that it needs to know where you are and still wants to look at everything else. So instead of "checking in" by glancing in your direction, they will lean to feel where you are so they don't have to look at you. If this begins to happen, you will need to start doing some very tight left hand turns directly into your dogs front end so they back off from you and begin to replace feeling you with looking at you.

During this process, I am usually talking to the dog constantly. I'm giving them a steady stream of verbal feedback about what they are doing. I'm trying to make it as easy as possible for them to keep their attention on me by talking to them a lot. Every time they stop the glancing in my direction, I surprise them with a turn, especially when I can see that their attention has shifted to something else. If they are walking next to me where I want them, I'm saying "Good Boy" or "Good Girl", occasionally petting them as I walk and stopping to pet them frequently as well. If they are too short to pet while I'm walking,

I'll stop more frequently to praise them for staying next to me. Stopping to pet them frequently is very important. We want to convey that being next to us is a very comfortable spot. That it is a safe spot for them because everything always goes well when they are there.

I must stress here that the point of this exercise is to demonstrate that you are the leader. Notice I said demonstrate. The most important part of this exercise are the turns. Most people that have a dog that pulls compete with their dog for leading on a walk. It looks something like this... A person and their dog are walking down the street with the dog at their side and the dog moves ahead and starts to pull. The person usually then does one of the following: a) The person jerks on the leash to slow the dog down, b) The person stops walking altogether until the dog stops pulling, c) the person just puts up with it, d) the person tries a halti or gentle leader or different type of training collar or harness, or e) The person tries to keep the dog from pulling by carrying treats everywhere. Unfortunately, none of these choices work very well to demonstrate that you are the leader. Nor do any of these methods lead to an attentive dog off of the leash later as does the turning to stay the leader. Think of it this way... instead of competing for the lead with your dog, be smarter than your dog. All it takes to be the leader again is to turn your back to the dog and start walking in a new direction. When this is done over and over again, your dog learns that the only way the walk progresses anywhere is if they let you lead the way.

Let's look at the other alternatives one at a time. In the first scenario, the dog pulls ahead and you snap on the leash to make them stop pulling and back up to where they should be walking next to you. If you snap on the leash hard enough, your dog will slow down and walk next to you for a short while. The action of snapping on the leash is a positive punishment, given because your dog is pulling your arm out of its socket. If you praise your dog for then walking next to you and not pulling, you've added a positive reinforcement for that action. But if there is something up ahead of you that your dog really wants to go and see, your dog will most likely be forging out ahead again within a very short time. You'll then repeat the process again and again. This comes down to competing with your dog for the lead of the walk. It's also important to realize that your dog may think that by forging ahead, they are actually getting to their desired destination sooner since you never stop moving towards the object of their interest. First, you're leading, then your dog is leading, then you're leading again and then your dog is leading again, and so on and so on. One positive thing about this approach is that your dog may begin to watch you a little more than they were before because they become wary of when you might snap the leash again. However, that is not the reason we want them to pay more attention to us. We want them to see us as the leader and pay attention because they know we always know what's best for them. You'll see the difference in a moment.

In the second scenario, you stop walking until your dog stops pulling. In this case, you are demonstrating some leadership by controlling the walk. The walk simply doesn't proceed until the dog backs off. Here you are using negative punishment, taking away the reward of the walk temporarily. If you then praise your dog for walking next to you, you've added positive reinforcement for the behavior you want. My experience with this approach is that if something up ahead is very interesting, your dog will start pulling again almost immediately when you begin walking thus causing you to stop again. If you have great amounts of patience you may eventually get your dog to walk decently provided you stay far enough away from any stimulus that your dog finds very interesting.

Next, you simply put up with it. I don't need to say much here. Since dogs are great at following the rule if it isn't broke don't fix it, nothing will change until you change something or your dog just gets too old to pull any more.

In the fourth scenario, you decide to change the tool you are using to walk your dog. By switching to a head harness like a Gentle Leader, a Halti, a pinch collar or prong style collar, you will have more control over your dogs pulling. The design of these tools is such that it makes it more difficult for your dog to pull. Gentle Leaders and Halti's do this by controlling your dog from under their jaw. Pinch collars do this through a series of links attached together that pinch the dogs skin slightly when the collar tightens from being pulled on.

With any head harness your leash attaches to a ring under their jaw, which is attached to straps that go over the nose. It is definitely easier to control a dog with your leash attached to their nose than it is to control your dog with the leash attached to their neck. A dog's neck is a very strong set of muscles. For this reason, I have found that some dogs are still able to pull even when on the Gentle Leader or Halti although much less effectively than if they are walked on a buckle collar or harness.

The Gentle Leader and Halti use negative reinforcement to "control" the dog. I would hesitate to use the term "train" the dog here because we are not really training as much as we are simply controlling the dog with a powerful tool. Over a period of time, most dogs will develop the habit of walking on a loose leash and may eventually be able to walk with a normal collar replacing the head harness. One problem most people encounter with a head harness is that they are very annoying for the dog to wear. You must be patient to get the dog past wanting to take it off. Once you are over that hurdle it gets much easier. One advantage of a head harness is they may have a calming effect on the dog wearing it. This calming effect may stem from the dog being made to exhibit self control when on a head harness. Since head harnesses are a powerful tool, you can subdue almost any dog with one when they get crazy. This forcing of your will for your dog to control itself will generally have the effect of raising your status and having your dog looking up to you. You are able to come across as strong. This is a good thing.

The pinch or prong collar is another tool which makes it harder for the dog to pull effectively. A pinch collar works by tightening around the dogs neck as they start to pull. The harder the dog pulls, the tighter it gets, up to a point where it won't tighten any further. When sized correctly, it is a tool that can safely work well to control an unruly dog. When used correctly, it can safely help lead you to a well behaved dog on or off of the leash later on. I personally prefer the pinch collar to a head harness for training, but that's just me. I feel it is more versatile in how it can be used and it seems it is less annoying for a dog to wear. The problem with only changing the collar you use is that you will most likely still be competing with your dog and not demonstrating clear leadership. There are some exceptions to my preference of a pinch collar over a head harness. These are usually situations where a very large dog is being walked by a very small or older person or if a dog is prone to trying to bite, I may choose a head harness over a pinch collar.

The last scenario uses treats to keep the dog walking next to you. The problem here is that treats are what the dog is paying attention to and if you happen to come across something that is really interesting to your dog, you may find yourself waving treats under your dog's nose and your dog showing no interest in them at all... until the distraction disappears and then of course your dog will want them again. Or, you may find that your dog won't walk well if they are not hungry.

Although I use treats in a lot of my training, I prefer not to use treats for teaching a dog to walk calmly on a loose leash. I find that treats actually interfere with teaching the dog to pay attention to me. If I'm holding treats in my hand the dog, is interested in the treats not in me. I want the dog to be attentive to me because they want to know where I am, not because they know I have treats. What happens if you don't have treats? You get the point.

Now, let's discuss a way to show leadership while at the same time teaching your dog to walk calmly next to you when on the heel command. You can actually use almost any type of collar for this exercise provided it won't pull over the dog's head if they were to resist and pull back from you. For this and other reasons, I avoid using a buckle collar to teach walking.

Begin with your dog on the side that you want to walk them on, holding the leash tight in your hands but with slack in the leash between you and your dog. You should have enough slack that your dog can move about 12 to 18 inches in any direction without feeling the leash pull on them. Imagine that there is a rectangular box on the ground next to you that your dog is supposed to stay inside of. As long as your dog stays within the boundaries of this imaginary box, everything proceeds comfortably. The moment your dog exits the box, you will do the opposite of your dog. If your dog moves ahead of you, which I define by watching if their feet are landing ahead of where mine are landing, you will do an about turn in the opposite direction of the side your dog walks on. For instance, if your dog is on your left, you will do an about turn to the right. As your dog continues in the direction they were headed the leash will pull tight and force the dog to go in the new direction you are headed. If your dog pulls to the left, you will go right. By doing the opposite of your dog whenever they move out of the imaginary box, you are demonstrating leadership. All you have to do to be the leader is turn your back and go in another direction. When you do this you are back in front of your dog. The type of training tool you use is not as important as the turning and staying in the leader position is, although, using a pinch or choke chain collar will generally work more effectively and be safer than using a buckle collar. When you examine all that is happening when you use this approach, you'll see the following... First, there is a positive punishment when the collar or other tool tightens and your dog

117

gets pulled in the new direction you are going. Secondly, there is a negative punishment as your dog is now being taken away from whatever it is that's up ahead that made them begin to pull. They are going to lose out on getting to go closer if they try to speed up the process of getting there. Thirdly, you will praise your dog the entire time they are walking where you want them to be walking giving them positive reinforcement for staying in the right place. Finally, you may even use negative reinforcement occasionally if your dog resists going in the new direction because they are so interested in what was up ahead of them. This would really only be the case though if you are using a tool that allows for this.

As you can see, we are able to use all of the different ways to change behavior in the above scenario creating a change quickly and permanently in how your dog walks with you, while at the same time demonstrating clear leadership. There are even some additional benefits as you'll soon see which lead to a well behaved and controllable dog off-leash later.

After making a turn in a new direction, I walk about 10 feet and then turn back in the direction I was going before. This gives your dog the opportunity to try pulling ahead again. If your dog pulls ahead, you will repeat the process. If they don't, you'll take them closer to what they are interested in if something is there drawing their attention away from you.

Heeling gives us an opportunity to begin to reinforce the word "NO" or whatever negative marker you use with your dog. Every time the leash and collar are about to pull on your dog because you are changing directions, you should say the word "No" or your replacement word for "No". You will have many opportunities to make your negative marker very important heeling your dog in this way. Remember to put the word directly preceding the pull on the leash and collar and you will be building up a strong response to the word you've chosen to mean "that's not allowed".

Let's recap again what is actually happening in this process. First of all, when we turn and go the opposite way, there will be a quick positive punishment when the leash tightens and the collar pulls on your dog. Secondly, the dog also finds they are now being taken away from whatever it is that drew their attention in the first place. This is the use of negative punishment. The dog is not getting to go towards the object of their interest. Thirdly, when the dog decides to stick close to me, to avoid the jerk on the leash when I change directions, they find that they get praised. But even more than that, they also get to keep moving closer to whatever they are interested in. These are both good positive reinforcements. If the distraction is safe, I'll then allow the dog to go over to it. The end result is that the dog understands that their best shot or chance at getting to go over to the things they are interested in is by staying close to me and letting me lead them. You should always be aware of what your dog is showing interest in while you are out walking. Giving your dog an opportunity to visit when they have shown self control and stayed close is one of the best rewards you have at your disposal, but you won't know what your dog is thinking if you don't keep an eye out for what is grabbing your dog's interest.

Another reason I like this approach is because in essence, it's the dog's fault that all of this happens. What I mean by that is your dog will only be able to know what you're going to do next if they stay where they can see you easily... next to your side. When they are in front of you, they can not know what you are going to do next because they can't see you easily. This makes it very easy for your dog to take responsibility for the way things play out. When they are in a position where they can't keep an eye on you, things go poorly. When they are next to you where they can see you, things go well.

Once your dog has taken responsibility for staying next to you, you'll notice that your dog is glancing in your direction regularly. This glancing at you is important for you to pay attention to. Instead of praising your dog for simply walking in the right place, take notice of the moments your dog glances at you and time your verbal praise marker, "Good Boy" or whatever you use, to be said at those moments when your dog glances at you to make sure you are still there next to them. By timing the marker at those moments, you'll be refining your dog's attention more and more with every walk.

You may even notice at times that your dog looks at you without looking away. If this happens, lay the verbal praise on extra thick and lavish until the moment something draws your dog's attention away from you again, and then right at that moment change direction on your dog, even if they are not out of place. This sudden change of direction timed right as your dog looks away from such a high level of attention will help to lock in to your dog's mind the importance of keeping an eye on you and how everything goes so well when they are watching you, the leader.

The heeling exercise is the foundation to having a dog that behaves, pays attention and listens well off-leash later. It may also be an exercise that helps to break through your dog's resistance to you being higher status and greatly contribute to getting rid of other problem behaviors as well.

Down Command

Perhaps the most important of all commands for the majority of dogs is the "down" command. Having your dog comply with the "down" command when asked, which means to lie down regardless of what is going on around them, can have a huge impact on how well your dog listens overall. I find that for about two thirds of the dogs I train, this will be the "breakthrough exercise". The act of lying down has the implication of admitting submission to you. Submission is not something most problem dogs will readily admit. Dogs with a huge resistance to lying down on command may even try to bite the person who is trying to make them comply. The down command hits a "home run" when it comes to getting the point across that you will be the leader. If your leadership has been questionable up this point and you have a dog you believe may be prone to trying to bite, you may want to get some professional help, otherwise proceed with caution to stay safe.

When I am working with a dog I feel is questionable in terms of safety, I will use two leashes to stay safe. One leash is attached to a collar on the dog that is then attached to a stationary object like a tree or something similar, and then the other leash is held by me and is attached to the training collar I am using on that dog. The leash attached to the tree will keep the dog from coming towards me should they decide to lash out and try to bite when I deliver a consequence for not listening. Keep in mind I am talking about a dog that knows what the "down" command means here and that this is generally not how I teach the down command. I usually use treats first to teach the dog what the command means, but as I mentioned earlier, doing a command for treats does not bring out the meaning of the command in the same way as asking for it without food rewards involved. When you first make the switch to giving the commands and you are no longer going to use treats, you will usually see the dog do the command for you a few times. Then, when it suddenly hits them that the treats are not coming after several times doing the command, they stop doing it. They stop doing it because the meaning of the command starts to emerge and they don't want to admit submission to you.

I did a consultation for a family with a three year old German Shepherd that was showing a lot of aggressive behavior. The dog had bitten people including family members which I did not know prior to visiting the people. To warm up to the dog I had some hot dogs which I used to help take the focus off of me as a trespasser on their property. After speaking with the people for a while about the dog's behavior and about behavior in general we went outside in their front yard to work with the dog. I asked if the dog knew the "down" command and got conflicting answers from the members of the family. My experience told me that the dog most likely knew the command being a three year old dog, especially since some of the family said the dog did know the command. In fact, most dogs over one year old I work with know exactly what the basic commands "sit" and "down" are, but are refusing to do them except when they feel there is something in it for them like a treat. This dog, I felt, was no exception. After all, German Shepards are very intelligent dogs and the family had attempted to teach the dog themselves prior to my showing up.

To test the dog's knowledge I took a piece of hot dog and lowered it in my hand to the ground under the dog's nose. The dog was sitting and bent slightly down but stopped almost immediately and would not go any further. I quickly took the treat away and tried again to lure the dog down as I said the command. The dog again refused to go down and I took the treat away again for a couple of seconds. The third time I did this, the dog tried to bite my hand to get the treat without doing the down. The husband of the family was holding the dog back from being able to come at me when this happened and the treat went flying across the yard. When the dog didn't get his treat for free, he lunged at me again very aggressively attempting to bite me and snagged my shirt with his canine tooth. We then changed gears and put the dog on the second leash and hooked him up to a post. I then had the husband, for whom the dog had the most respect of anyone, try and gently pull the dog's front legs out and then gently lower the dog into the down position. In doing so, the dog resisted and bit the hand of the owner. After attempting several other ways to get the dog to do the down command and watching the level of aggression that this dog had and what the dog was willing to try to keep from doing the "down" I recommended that they put the dog to sleep. This dog knew exactly what "down" meant and was not about to do it for anyone. It wasn't necessarily that this

124

dog couldn't be trained, but after working with thousands of dogs, I felt that this dog was just too great a risk to have in a family with young kids who had friends coming over, especially since he had bitten the wife several times in the past and he had no bite control whatsoever. When he bit, he did damage to whomever he was biting. In a different home, I may have had a different assessment, but not in a family with children.

Admittedly, I am not as conservative as many trainers. In fact, it is rare that I tell a customer to put a dog to sleep. Over the years, I have helped many families with dogs that other trainers had said to have the dog put to sleep without ever seeing the dog first hand. I make it a point to see a dog before I tell someone to end the dog's life and this policy has saved many dogs from death row that simply needed a little feedback about their behavior to be good family dogs. Getting back to the German Shepard, this dog truly was a time bomb ready to go off anytime someone pressured him do something he didn't feel like doing. After the incident and attempts we made in the front yard to get the dog to comply with the down command, the wife and husband told me the dog had bitten both of them in the past when they had tried to make the dog move or go somewhere he didn't want to go. They had not told me this prior to the session. They had only told me about the incidents that had happened with visitors to their home. Once all the information came out, it was clear this dog was not safe in this household for sure and I made my recommendation.

I tell that story because I want to emphasize how much meaning there is behind the "down" command and to stress that if your own dog is highly resistant to doing "down" for you, to please be careful and get professional help. This doesn't mean you need to rush out and put your dog to sleep if they lash out when you try to make them comply with the command. I find that once you get over the hump of having the dog do the first few "downs" for you and the dog starts to comply with ease that the dog's attitude will usually change tremendously. I offered to help these people even though I told them I thought the dog was dangerous and should be put down. I can't make someone put their dog to sleep and I know how big an impact training can have on a dog so I made the offer. The people told me they would think about it but I think they had already decided to put the dog to sleep after seeing how something as small as not getting a treat could set their dog off.

The "down" command exercise will be the most difficult for most dogs to comply with. It is the exercise that will bring out the most resistance from the dog and shape how the dog looks at you more than any other exercise for the majority of dogs. I tell my clients that down, for many dogs, is the "nucleus" to all the problems they are dealing with when their dog won't do the down command and that once their dog starts to do the down command for them, it becomes the "nucleus" to the rest of their training program, helping to keep their dog trained even when they are not using many of the other commands on a regular basis. It too is a breakthrough exercise.

When working on this exercise remember to stay aware and be safe if you have a dog that has shown any aggressive tendencies in the past.

Keeping with your pattern of not repeating yourself without putting closure to the previous command, you will ask your dog to "down". If your dog refuses, and you know they do know the command, you will follow through with a negative consequence. Generally, I use a leash and collar correction for this. I give one command and then I give one consequence. If the dog complies, the consequence is comforting praise and petting and/or the very occasional surprise treat for an exceptional response. If the dog doesn't comply, I give a negative consequence. I make a big deal about the first few times the dog complies because IT IS a big deal to get them to comply those first few times.

Once your dog is willing to comply in the setting of your house and yard, you will take your training outside. This is where the bulk of the meaning will come into play. Your job at this point is to put your dog into situations where they have a choice. You will ask for a "down" when something else has taken their attention away from you. For instance, ask your dog for a "down" when they are watching a person across the street getting out of their car, or when they are observing the squirrel on the ground 20 feet away. The more different choices you put your dog into, the quicker your dog will generalize that they need to do the command no matter what they are watching. This is the priority rearrangement phase of your dog's lessons.

Most dogs will eventually get to the point where they can observe the interesting things going on in the world around them and listen to your commands. In other words, you ask for a "down" while your dog is staring at a cat and without looking away from the cat your dog complies with your command. There is nothing wrong with this, so don't worry if you see this happening. Your dog doesn't have to look at you to comply.

In fact, don't ever worry about what your dog is looking at when you want to give them a command. Your dog doesn't need to be looking at you to be able to hear you. For some reason, I find that a lot of people want to say their dog's name first and wait until their dog looks at them before they give the dog a command. I find this practice will actually have the effect of teaching your dog to ignore you more, instead of listen better. Think about it for a moment. Let's say that you say your dog's name to get them to look at you and when they do, you then you tell them to do something that takes them away from what they were doing. And if they don't look at you, you don't give them a command until they do look at you. I can guarantee you that the end result of this scenario when repeated over and over will be that your dog ignores their name and won't turn to look at you. My guess is that you would do the exact same thing if every time someone said your name and you turned to look and were then told to do something you didn't want to do. You would eventually get to the point where you don't want to acknowledge your name too. Your dog is smart enough to figure out that pattern very quickly.

Stay Command

We've covered the two most important commands that create breakthroughs in your relationship with your dog. The next command we'll discuss is the "stay command". There is another powerful message behind the "stay command". In essence, you are controlling your dog's space.

In a pack of dogs, the lead or top dogs control space and have the lower status members of the pack yield to them. That is to say, the lower status dogs get out of the way of the higher status dogs when they are moving around. They get up and move from preferred resting spots, they eat second and when they are disciplined by higher status dogs, they are sometimes made to stay in one place with their head lowered to the ground until the top dog allows them to get up and move around again. Does your dog get out of your way when you begin to walk in their direction or will they just lie there and have you walk around them? Does your dog stay put when you give them a command not to move?

If you are in the habit of walking around your dog you need to change your behavior. Stop being so nice and polite to your dog. By trying not to disturb your dog when they seem comfortable, you are sending a message that they get to control space. Since you are the one yielding to them you will appear to be lower status to your dog. This will greatly contribute to a dog not listening and obeying your commands. A dog will not readily listen to someone that they have determined to be of lower status than they are. Start making your dog get out of your way when you are about to walk around them or step over them. Make them move to a different spot if they are sitting in the best spot. And here's a hint: in the beginning, they always have the best spot. In some homes, this one change may make a big difference.

The "stay command" is another way of controlling space. Like making your dog yield to you when you are moving around. Making your dog stay put while you move around has a very strong message behind it too. It still boils down to controlling space, just in a different way. Here we are telling the dog that this small space you are on is the only space I'm allowing you to be on at this time. You cannot move. This is especially helpful when you are trying to get your dog to listen better inside of your house. Do down stays in every room, the back yard, the front yard, etc. By doing this exercise in all of the areas where you live with your dog, you will be helping your dog to generalize that you are higher status everywhere.

On the same note, not allowing your dog to have access to certain areas of the house or yard will help to get this message across even better. Even if you eventually want to let your dog roam your entire house freely, it is extremely helpful to disallow access to some areas when you are trying to get your dog to listen better. You can always allow access later when your dog has gotten the message that you run the house and that they must listen.

To recap, the basic commands that will have an impact on how your dog views you are Heel, Down, Come, and Stay. And of course, you'll also teach the convenience command, Sit. By teaching all of these basic commands and then using them on a regular basis in environments where you are giving your dog choices, especially difficult ones, you will be moving forward towards your goal of having a dog that listens with great reliability as well as building a bond and strengthening your relationship.

Chapter Eight

Tools of the Trade

There are a variety of tools available to train dogs. Most of these tools are available from your local pet stores and have already been discussed throughout the book. Tools help us in several ways to be more clear with our dog. Depending on the tool being discussed, it might help us to be more precise with our timing, to enable us to remove ourself from the situation so our presence is not an influence in the learning, to alert us to our dog's behavior when we are nearby but not watching them, to help us to deliver a consequence that might otherwise be difficult to deliver, such as when the dog is at a distance from us or we are separated from our dog by an obstacle like a wall or door, etc. Tools also help us to be consistent and consistency is

132

the name of the game in dog training.

As a trainer, I have used most of the tools out there at some point over the years. I have found most of them have a time and place where their use is warranted and if used properly, are safe. Depending on the situation, there might be several tools that can work in helping you to solve a problem or teach something new to your dog. Let me begin by dividing tools into three categories. First, we have the tools that help us to teach something new to our dog. Second, we have those tools that help us to stop our dog from doing something we don't want them to do. And third, we have those tools which help us manage situations or behavior.

Let's start with the first group that helps us to teach something new to our dog. The most commonly used tool for teaching a dog something new is food. You may not think of food as a tool, but in reality, when you are raising a puppy or have taken in a rescue dog that needs training, food can either be your ally in training or it can undermine your efforts if used incorrectly. The correct use of food or treats can help to strengthen behavior. It's when food is given freely without getting something back from your dog that it begins to undermine your efforts. Dogs that are highly motivated by food are perhaps the easiest to train. A high quality treat can help to keep a dog focused and get them to try harder. And don't assume that all treats are equal and just because your dog seems to enjoy a particular treat, that it is good enough. I've had hundreds of situations where a dog that liked a particular treat, according to their owners, wasn't motivated enough for me to consider it to be a good enough treat. Most of the time in those situations if I grab some lunch meat or cheese from the fridge, it will become apparent how much difference there can be between different types of treats.

Another tool used to teach new things to your dog is a "clicker". A clicker is a small tool that makes a click sound when pressed. It is used to mark behavior accurately. It is the same thing as saying "good dog" or something similar. The advantage of the clicker is that the click is shorter than saying "good dog" and more accurately pinpoints the moment the dog has completed the behavior you are working on. It also sounds the same no matter who is doing the clicking, making it easier for your dog to be learning from more than one person. If you are paying attention and trying to mark very accurately a behavior, the clicker is probably the best tool available to help speed up your dog's learning a new behavior. I also find that a dog tends to learn new behaviors more quickly after they get "in tune" with what the click means. It's as if they are on a learning curve and as they get better at understanding that they are causing the click by something they are doing, they get very in tune with paying close attention to what they are doing the moment they hear the click.

Another tool that may be useful is a toy that the dog loves. A toy used for reward can be an excellent tool, especially when you have a dog that isn't very food motivated. Throwing a ball or squeaky toy after they perform a command for you can make all the work seem like play to your dog and to you too.

The above tools are the main ones I use for teaching new behaviors. In the case where I am working with a dog that is not motivated by any food or toys, we use praise as the main reward. Praise will work nearly every time because it is the only reward that you have the ability to create an opposite of. In other words, you can create a feeling of discomfort as a contrast to make the praise/comfort you are giving stand out even more. This will work on virtually every dog if everything else fails to be rewarding enough.

Now we're going to talk about the tools of the trade that help create the discomfort that will contribute to stopping unwanted behaviors and refine your dog's listening. We've already discussed some of the different collars that can be used to deliver consequences. There are choke chain collars, pinch collars, head halters of many varieties, electronic training collars for off-leash and even on-leash work. As I said earlier, they all have their place. You need to find the tools that work best for you and your dog. A trainer who is familiar with all of the tools will be able to help you should you find yourself confused or frustrated about which one you should use. Generally, I find that the tool has to be matched to both the person and the dog. The person has to be comfortable using the tool or it won't get used, and at the same time, it has to be effective on the dog.

For example, I have trained many dogs over the years whereone tool outshined all the others on a particular dog. I once was training a Rhodesian Ridgeback that, when on an electronic collar, was able to ignore the sensation even on the highest setting and when we switched to a pinch collar, started working like a soldier. On the other hand, I remember a silky terrier I was once training that would get so amped up when on a walk that a pinch collar was useless. You could have yanked the leash hard enough to make the dog do a back flip and it wouldn't have even noticed it and would be instantly back to whatever it was focused on. In this case the pinch collar or choke chain collar was not only useless it was dangerous, because it was ineffective at the maximum level I thought it could be safely used. Yet this dog was super sensitive to an electronic collar. I had the collar set so low the sensation was undetectable to me or the owner at the level the dog responded to. My point here is that you should never be afraid to try a different tool if the one you are using is not working well on your dog. Continuing to do the same thing over and over again expecting a different result is one definition of insanity.

There are also tools that I use to booby trap a dog so I am alerted to them doing something they shouldn't be doing when I am out of the room. One tool I use often is a vibration sensitive door alarm made by Techko. This tool can be picked up at stores like Home Depot in the home alarm department. With a bit of ingenuity, it can tell you when your dog is doing something they shouldn't be doing even if you are not in the immediate area, but are close by, thus allowing you to stay consistent. This alarm emits a very loud, ear piercing noise when moved after it has "armed" itself. By setting the alarm on a couch that your dog is getting on when you are not in the room, you will know the instant the dog jumps up on the couch and disturbs the alarm, thus allowing you to catch them in the act even though you are not present.

Finally, we have those tools that help us to manage our dogs. These tools consist of items like dog crates, dog runs, head harnesses, jump harnesses, etc.

Crates and dog runs definitely have their place in training. Crates and runs allow you to control your dog's space when you are not around to give them feedback about their behavior. This is important since dogs can easily learn that something is okay to do when you are not around and only dangerous to do if you are around.

Giving your dog access to things they are damaging and/or places you don't want them going when you are not around is a sure fire way to undermine your training efforts. It may well be the number one mistake that new dog owners make. Puppies and adult dogs too need to earn their right to have freedom to roam your house. More freedom is given, a little at a time, when your dog has been behaving well for several weeks. Freedom to roam in your absence is first given for very short time periods and is gradually expanded over time as your dog has shown his ability to stay out of mischief in your absence.

Chapter Nine

Consistency is Key

In the last chapter, I mentioned that probably the biggest mistake of all I see when visiting homes is that people give their dog more freedom than their dog has earned the right to have at that point in their training and living with them. Freedom to roam the house is not a right, it is a privilege which is earned by showing consistently good behavior. Freedom to roam without supervision is given on a gradual basis. As your dog demonstrates that he is able to behave responsibly, you will give your dog more freedom a little at a time.

Just to be clear, it is better to have your dog crated, in an exercise pen or kenneled if you are unable to supervise your dog while they are still learning the rules and boundaries you are working to establish. If you are around and can have your dog with you, you can have them do a long down stay while you attend to something else like working on the computer, watching tv, etc. In fact, doing a lot of down stays will have a substantial calming effect on many dogs and make dealing with them much easier.

Giving your dog too much freedom too quickly is without a doubt the easiest way to undermine your efforts. Since consistency is the key to dog training, it becomes obvious right away that giving freedom or access to things and places that are still problems for your dog when you are not around is the biggest mistake you can make.

Earlier in the book I talked about how punishments need to be delivered with a high level of consistency to be effective or the reward your dog gets out of doing the unwanted behavior becomes intermittent and variable and will most likely overpower your punishments. Fully understanding this concept will help get you over the idea that you are confining your dog if it bothers you.

Keep in mind too that you will only be doing this for a short time. And it's natural for dogs to be den bound while they are very young. Mother dogs keep their pups close to the den where they can be protected and safe. Many dogs enjoy using their crate for their entire life. It is not jail like some people seem to think. It is more like a bedroom for your dog. They just don't need as much space as we do. Many dogs are actually more content and comfortable when left in their crate when you leave than they are having full freedom to roam your house.

When you are at home, you want to be consistent with your dog then as well. Not being prepared for things your dog might do is perhaps the second biggest mistake I see people make. It is quite easy to stay consistent if you are using the right tools. To stay consistent at home, you need to keep a leash and training collar or an electronic training collar on your dog whenever they are in the house with you until you find that you don't need it any longer. I find that many times people who know that their dog is still with challenges will undermine their efforts by putting their dog in a situation where they have no ability to follow through on what their dog may do, before they have seen their dog perform consistently in that situation with the ability to follow through on their actions.

For instance, if you have decided to use a remote training collar, you should put it on first thing in the morning and it should stay on throughout the entire day until bedtime when it comes off and goes back on it's charger to be ready for the next day. Many times, simply having the collar on your dog will help your dog to behave better. The most important thing to know about that effect is it helps with the habit forming process. If your dog behaves better because you have their collar on them and you do this consistently even though you may rarely be using the collar to deliver a consequence, you are helping habits to form. After 2 to 3 months of doing this consistently and following through if necessary whenever you have the opportunity, you should have a dog that you can count on to listen in almost any situation if not perfectly.

Chapter Ten

Breaking Your Bad Habits

So now it's time to implement everything you've been learning. To do this, you will need to break your habits of how you have been dealing with your dog up to now. The hardest thing of all is to stay consistent with the principles you've been learning here. Below is a list of the things that I find most people will likely fall short on:

1. Restrict freedom to roam when you can't be watching your dog.

2. Keep those things booby trapped that you want left alone until your dog has not touched them for over one month.

3. Always walk your dog with their training collar on until you have been on dozens of walks where your dog behaved responsibly even when confronted with major distractions.

4. Keep a leash and collar or electronic training collar on your dog when in your house so that you can deliver a consequence promptly until it has become obvious that he doesn't need it any more.

5. If using an electronic collar, put it on in the morning and take it off before bedtime each night, every day until you have not had to use it for over two months.

6. When giving commands to your dog, do not repeat yourself until you have given closure to the command you just gave.

7. Build a new habit of using the same commands each time and stop trying to say the same thing in every different way that you know how to.

8. Build a new habit of saying all of your commands in a friendly tone without raising your voice.

9. Pay attention to your body language and use it to help get across the message of what your words mean.

10. Eliminate the use of visual cues for the time being until you can see that your dog is listening when you ask them to do something and then add them back later putting them in front of the verbal cue if you want your dog to learn visual cues.

11. Take your dog out on regular walks to stimulate their mind, satisfy their socialization needs, help shape the way they view you, and give them exercise.

12. When your dog is in the house with you, control the living space and make your dog do frequent "down stays" in all areas of the house. If you have a particularly difficult dog, bombard them with "down stays".

13. Ask your dog to do something for you every time you are going to do something for them because nothing in life is free.

14. Apply consequences every time you have an opportunity and the resources to do so. This is consistency.

By following these basic principles you will begin to see a new dog emerge from the old difficult one, many times in as little as a few days. You'll notice more attentiveness, calmness that wasn't present before, quicker, more reliable responses where there was no response at all in the past, and problems disappearing permanently.

The end result will be a dog that you will remember as being a great family companion many years after they have passed on. And with each new canine addition to your house, you'll get better at applying what you've learned here and find it easier and easier to raise a well-behaved dog without getting stressed out.

So stop stressing out and get started. It's time to get to work.

Made in the USA
Middletown, DE
02 July 2020

10755707R00084